BEING MY BEST
FOR GOD

KENT GARBORG

BroadStreet
PUBLISHING

BroadStreet Publishing Group, LLC
Racine, Wisconsin, USA
BroadStreetPublishing.com

BEING MY BEST FOR GOD

Written by Kent Garborg with Debra Klingsporn

ISBN-13: 978-1-4245-5395-2 (faux leather)
ISBN-13: 978-1-4245-5396-9 (e-book)

Stock or custom editions of BroadStreet Publishing titles may be purchased in bulk for educational, business, ministry, fundraising, or sales promotional use. For information, please e-mail info@broadstreetpublishing.com.

Cover design by Chris Garborg at www.garborgdesign.com.
Typesetting by Katherine Lloyd at www.theDESKonline.com.

Printed in China
17 18 19 20 21 5 4 3 2 1

To Hudson Trygve Gorrie,
our first grandchild.
It was our love for each other
that fanned the spark of this
idea into a flame.

A NOTE TO PARENTS

These daily readings were inspired by the classic Christian devotional *My Utmost for His Highest* by Oswald Chambers.[*] If I could only have one other book besides the Bible, it would be *My Utmost*. If you don't have a copy of the original devotional, I urge you to get ahold of one and begin reading it daily.

Several years ago, while wondering how to get my own children and grandchildren exposed to the deeper truths of the Christian gospel, the idea for this book came to mind. I spent four months reading and re-reading the words of Chambers. Then I began writing down thoughts that were sparked by each selection. In some cases these thoughts paralleled Chambers' ideas, only in a language I hoped would be easier for children to grasp.

In other cases, ideas were sparked in my mind that were not directly aligned with the teaching of *My Utmost*. They moved in a different yet complementary direction. In some cases, my writings may not even seem to agree completely with the theology expressed in *My Utmost for His Highest*. I'm not a theologian, and so that was not intentional.

---

[*] If you do not know who Oswald Chambers is or are unfamiliar with his work, pick up a copy of *Oswald Chambers: Abandoned to God: The Life Story of the Author of My Utmost for His Highest*, by David McCasland (Discovery House Publishers, Grand Rapids, MI).

When the project was complete, I asked my friend Debra Klingsporn to write a prayer or activity for each daily selection. She did a marvelous job. Her prayers added an element I felt necessary to assist readers in applying the daily message to their lives. I think you'll agree.

Two final comments: First, some of these selections will stretch young readers. They may struggle to understand the truths presented. All I can say is that Chambers' original work still stretches me as an adult. I read his devotionals over and over, year after year, and they continue to challenge me. I hope your kids will do the same.

Second, I encourage you to be reading *My Utmost* as your child is reading *Being My Best for God*. I believe this practice will lead to profound discussions of some very deep issues that may enlighten both you and your child. Furthermore, if you are processing the daily readings by Chambers, you will be better able to assist your child in coming to a deeper understanding of God's ways.

May God bless you and bless your child as you take this journey together.

—Kent Garborg

JANUARY

THE MOST
IMPORTANT THING

May these words of my mouth and this meditation
of my heart be pleasing in your sight, LORD.

Psalm 19:14

Knowing God and finding out how he wants me to live
is the most important thing in life.

Because God is God, being my best to please him is
what life is all about. I may want to please my friends, my
teachers, or my parents, and that's okay. I just don't want
to worry more about what others think of me than what my
heavenly Father thinks. He is the most important.

If I want to be my best for God, I will not always
demand what I want when I want it. He will give me the
patience to wait for his perfect will and timing. And if I will
learn to be patient, he will put his desires in my heart. That
means he'll help me want what he wants for me. Then it
will be easy to please him. I'll want what he wants, and he'll
give me the patience to wait for his best.

God, I'm not really sure I know what "knowing you"
means. It would be so much easier if you were right
here in front of me. Help me learn what being my best
to please you really means. I want to know you, God.
Amen.

WHAT'S NEXT?

Trust in the Lord with all your heart and lean not on
your own understanding; in all your ways submit to him,
and he will make your paths straight.

Proverbs 3:5–6

The secret to trusting God is believing the truth about
him and about me. The truth about God is that he is
completely loving and dependable. He will never fail me.
The truth about me is that I am created to totally depend
on this loving and totally dependable God.

If I really believe God is who he says he is—all loving,
wise, and powerful—I never need to worry. I may not
always know what is going to happen or what I am
supposed to do next, but God knows what is coming. He
knows everything! He can do anything! I can trust him
completely and forever!

God, I don't always know what's coming next.
Sometimes I'm scared about many different things, but
I'm going to trust you. The Bible tells me to trust you
even when I'm not sure what *you* are doing in my life,
so today, I'm going to trust in your love, knowing I can
count on that no matter what. Amen.

STUMPED?

Now I know in part; then I shall know fully,
even as I am fully known.

1 Corinthians 13:12

Sometimes life is hard to figure out. I may go through a confusing experience. I might feel like I'm in the dark, and I don't know where to turn or what to think. God wants to use those times to show me how great he is and how much he loves me. He wants to prove to me that he can be trusted.

God is God! I will never completely figure him out. That's why he sent Jesus, a human being just like me. Jesus is God's picture of himself. The more I get to know Jesus, the clearer my picture of God will be. If my picture of God is clear, I will still trust him even when I am confused about life. In time he will give me all the understanding I need.

— — — — —

God, I want to know you, but sometimes when I pray it feels like nobody is listening. Sometimes the Bible has a lot of confusing words and weird phrases that don't make much sense to me. Does faith mean trusting you with everything I don't know and believing that one day all my confusion will be gone? I hope so, God, because I know you love me and you're with me. And that's enough for today. Amen.

GOD'S ANSWERS

Take delight in the LORD, and he will give you
the desires of your heart. Commit your way to the LORD;
trust in him and he will do this: Be still before
the LORD and wait patiently for him.

Psalm 37:4–5, 7

God doesn't always answer my prayers right away. That doesn't mean the answer is "No."

It might mean God wants me to learn patience. Learning to be patient means knowing God is always right on time. God never answers too early or too late. Whenever God says, "Wait," it is usually because he wants to do something in me, to teach me something. That is more important than immediately giving me what I want.

Whenever I get impatient and try to run ahead of God, I stumble. I want to learn to wait. I want to learn that what God is doing inside of me—in my character—is more important than what is happening outside of me and in my circumstances. I want to kick back and relax in the knowledge that God is always right on time.

———

God, if answers to my prayers don't come quickly, help me be patient and wait. I know you will give me the desires of my heart, but not necessarily now and not necessarily all at once. Amen.

I'M GROWING

So that you may live a life worthy of the Lord and please
him in every way . . .
growing in the knowledge of God.

Colossians 1:10

To God, growing up isn't just getting bigger, stronger, smarter, and more able to take care of myself. Nor is it just not having to depend on my parents or teachers. Being grown up doesn't mean, "I can do it myself" or "I don't need anybody else."

Real growing up means knowing God better and understanding how dependent I am on him.

God's son, Jesus Christ, is the picture of a real grown-up. Jesus gives me an example of how to live completely depending on God. Real growing up means I am learning to be more and more dependent on my heavenly Father. If Jesus is God's example of what a real grown-up is like, then I want to learn how to live the same way he did.

God, I know I'm just a kid. There's a lot I don't know, but I do know growing up, both physically and spiritually, takes time, and that's okay. Today, I trust in you, and I trust that in time I'll understand you better. Amen.

I'M HANDMADE!

I praise you because I am fearfully and
wonderfully made; your works are wonderful,
I know that full well.

Psalm 139:14

E very talent or ability that I have is a gift from God.
Sometimes I may compare myself to others and
think, "I'm not very good at anything." When I do that, I'm
forgetting one very important thing: God made me just the
way I am. I may not know what I'm good at yet, but I know
I'm wonderfully made.

As I learn to trust God more, I begin to realize he made
me unique—not like anyone else. Since he made me the
way I am, I don't need to compare myself with anyone else.
I can just say, "Thanks for making me just the way I am!"

- - - -

Dear God, sometimes I think my friends are smarter,
more talented, or better at sports. But other times I
think I'm better than other kids. I know comparing
myself to other kids doesn't do me any good, but I still
do it. Forgive me when I do that. Help me remember
to be who you created me to be. Thank you, God, for
making me *me*! Amen.

A TRUE FRIEND

"I have called you friends, for everything that
I learned from my Father I have made known to you."

John 15:15

N ot only does God want me to know him as my Father,
but he also wants me to know him so well that we can
call each other friends. What do friends do? They hang out
together and talk about things. Real friends can talk about
anything. They have no secrets.

How do I let God be my friend? I can start by talking
about absolutely everything with him. When I try to keep
things hidden from God, it makes me uncomfortable
around him. Telling God about everything is called "living
in the light."

The Bible says, "God is Light." When I "live in the light,"
I'm living where God is. Then we are close, like friends. He
knows everything about me anyway, so I never need to be
embarrassed about being totally honest with him.

- - - - -

Thank you, God, for loving me. Even though sometimes
you seem too big to understand, thank you for sending
Jesus to be my friend and for caring about little stuff
(like a loose tooth) and big stuff (like being afraid of
the dark). Amen.

GOD FIRST

"Love the LORD your God with all your heart and with
all your soul and with all your strength and with
all your mind; and, Love your neighbor as yourself."

Luke 10:27

God wants our relationship to be more important than any other relationship. If there is anything in my life more important to me than God, it will keep me from enjoying the best friend I could ever have.

For example, I may have friends who try to keep me from being my best for God. Or I can put other things ahead of God. Slowly, I may notice that I don't want to spend as much time with God or that I don't feel I need to be honest with him about what I am thinking and doing.

If this begins to happen I will want to stop and take the time to be totally honest with my most important friend. I want to put my relationship with him first. God wants to be my best friend.

— — — —

Dear God, I'm not sure I know what it means to put you first. I'm almost afraid to ask you this, God, but does it mean you're supposed to be more important than *anything?* God, I don't think I can honestly say you really are more important to me than anything else. Help me know what it means to put you first—I don't think I've got that part down yet. Amen.

GOD KNOWS BEST

For it is God who works in you to will
and to act in order to fulfill his good purpose.

Philippians 2:13

The God who is my friend is the God who made everything—the early mornings, the late nights, the mountains, oceans, and sky, and every creature in them. God knows me better than I know myself because he made me too.

The reason I can surrender everything to him is because this incredibly great big God is my Father and my friend. He made me so that I would only be the happiest when I am the closest to him.

The deepest joy I can imagine is the joy of knowing him and being his friend. It's hard to imagine, but this Creator-God wants to hang out with me. Like a true best friend, he will show me how to live for him because that is why he created me.

— — — — —

Dear God, thank you for making big things like elephants, waterfalls, and trees. Thank you for little things like ladybugs, sparrows, blooming flowers, and falling snow. Thank you, God, that you are at work in everything I see and feel and smell and hear. Forgive me when I'm grouchy and when I whine about little stuff. I forget that compared to your big world, I really am pretty small. And yet you love me. Your love is bigger than anything I can imagine. Amen.

BEST FRIENDS FOREVER

I said, "I will confess my transgressions to the LORD."
And you forgave the guilt of my sin.

Psalm 32:5

When best friends keep secrets from each other, it hurts their relationship. The surest way I can protect my friendship with God is to tell him about everything, good or bad. Telling God everything is called "confession." Confession is just being truthful about everything I have said or thought or done.

Whenever I am sorry for my behavior and confess my failures to God, he forgives me. Being forgiven is like getting a gift. All I have to do is accept it and say, "Thank you."

It's a great feeling to be honest and to know there are no more secrets keeping me from enjoying my best friend's company.

— — — — —

God, forgiveness seems too easy. Is it really true that when I do something bad or when I hurt someone's feelings all I have to do is tell you and you'll forgive me? And there's another thing I don't understand about forgiveness. Why do I still feel bad even after I say I'm sorry or ask for forgiveness? Maybe what's hard isn't being forgiven but accepting forgiveness—and learning to forgive myself. Help me, God, learn to forgive myself. Amen.

MAKING GOD HAPPY

*"The one who sent me is with me; he has not
left me alone, for I always do what pleases him."*

John 8:29

E very day the most important thing is to do what
pleases God. When I understand that God is my best
friend, doing what pleases him will not be difficult. I would
want my best friend to be pleased with what I do. It is easy
to want to please someone you love. But sometimes if I put
God first, it might upset other people.

Some of my friends might not understand my
friendship with God. They may not think friendship with
God is important. They might not even want to be God's
friend. Even though I may be misunderstood, I want to
keep God first.

I pray that all my friends want to know him too. I always
want to do what pleases my heavenly Father, even though it
might cost me an earthly friendship.

— — — —

God, wanting to please you sounds so simple, but it
seems so hard sometimes. At school I hardly remember
to think of you. At home there's usually so much stuff
going on. When I'm in bed I usually remember to pray,
but a lot of times I don't know what to pray for. I really
do want to do what you want me to do. Today, God, help
me just remember to be grateful. Amen.

TALKING AND LISTENING

You, God, are my God, earnestly I seek you;
I thirst for you, my whole being longs for you.

Psalm 63:1

If God and I are truly best friends, we will want to spend time talking and listening to each other. The best way for this to happen is to set aside time to be alone with God each day. I will want to talk with him about whatever is on my heart and mind. But, I will also want to learn to listen.

Friendship with God is a two-way conversation. To hear what God has to say, I will need to be very quiet. Sometimes he will speak to me through his words in the Bible. Other times, I may hear him with "the ears of my heart." That means I won't hear God speaking out loud, but I will get a strong inner feeling or impression about something I need to do or something he wants me to know.

True friends are good listeners. I will learn to listen to God.

- - - -

God, I know some things take time. I can't rush a butterfly out of its cocoon or make wet paint dry faster. I'm guessing that learning to know you is one of those things that can't be rushed. But, God, sometimes I wish it could. Sometimes I wish I could hear your voice. But for now, here I am. Be with me. Help me learn what it means to listen for your voice. Amen.

MAKING THINGS CLEAR

Be still, and know that I am God.

Psalm 46:10

The longer I have a friendship with God, the better I will get to know him. The more I get to know him, the more time I will want to spend with him. The more time I spend with him, the more I will be able to hear his voice and learn how to live. And, yet, I will need to be patient with myself because it will take God some time to shape me into the person he created me to be.

Sometimes he will use unpleasant experiences, disappointments, sadness, and even sickness to teach me. He will also help me learn to listen. Even when I think I know God well, some things will still be confusing or painful. At those times, I will want to take the time to be alone with him.

I can ask for understanding or ask God to help me trust him, whether I understand or not.

— — — —

God, when I try to listen quietly, I still hear a lot of noise—everything from the refrigerator humming to the stereo or TV in another part of the house. If the only way I can learn to know you is by learning to be quiet, then I think I'm in trouble! God, the truth is, when I try to be quiet and pray, I'm antsy and restless and distracted by everything! I'm willing to be patient, but I could use a little help. Will you show me how to be still and know that you are God? Amen.

I'M LISTENING

Then I heard the voice of the LORD saying,
"Whom shall I send? And who will go for us?"
And I said, "Here am I. Send me!"

Isaiah 6:8

God will never force me to do anything. He never raises his voice to make me obey. He speaks softly. Whether or not I hear God speaking depends mainly on whether or not I am listening carefully. But it also depends on whether or not I am willing to obey him if he did speak to me. Do I really want to hear him? If I hear God speak, am I willing to obey him?

The people God chooses to do his work are those friends who are listening for his voice. His true friends have decided ahead of time, in their hearts, that they will do whatever he asks.

God is always calling me. Whether I hear him or not depends on whether my heart is saying, "Here I am!" The more willing I am to obey God, the more clearly I will hear his voice.

— — — —

God, are you "calling" me to do something today? Moses or David or even Mary could have said no instead of yes. I may not know what you want me to do with my life yet, but I know I want my response to be a big "Yes!" Create in me, O God, a willing heart. Amen.

DYING TO LIVE

Therefore, if anyone is in Christ, the new creation
has come: The old has gone, the new is here!

2 Corinthians 5:17

Sometimes I will want to have or do things I know would not please God. That is normal.

Yet just like Jesus died and rose again, God wants me to die to any desires that are not pleasing to him. If I am willing to do that, I will come alive to a different way of life—his way of wanting and thinking and doing.

Am I willing to let God's way be the only way? If I am, he will show me a new way of thinking and acting that is pleasing to him, even though it may seem uncomfortable to me at first. If I let him help me, obeying him will become as natural to me as breathing.

— — — — —

One of the greatest Christian teachers in the last hundred years, Oswald Chambers, said that being "new" in Christ was like having a "funeral" in our own honor. That means something like this: When a caterpillar spins a chrysalis, spinning the chrysalis is like having a funeral for the worm that he is. Asking Jesus to live in our hearts is like spinning a spiritual cocoon—we are asking Jesus to change us from the inside out. Then we can become the beautiful person God created us to be, just like a butterfly! Jesus, make me who you created me to be. Amen.

HEARING THE RIGHT VOICE

And let us run with perseverance the race
marked out for us, fixing our eyes on Jesus,
the pioneer and perfecter of faith.

Hebrews 12:1–2

God has a special purpose or "call" for my life. I can
easily miss God's call because there are so many other
voices calling me—so many other things that pull my
attention away from God.

The only way I will know God's call or purpose for my
life is by paying close attention, so I will hear God's gentle,
loving guidance.

Do I want to find the purpose for which God created
me? Or will I risk missing God's call because of the other
things I want to do instead?

— — — —

Dear God, it isn't always easy to tell when I'm choosing
to do things my way or your way. But I do know the
choices I make matter: now, today, wherever I am, and
whomever I'm with. They all matter to you. Help me
know the difference between godly choices (those that
please you) and selfish choices (those that might make
you sad). Amen.

UNWRAPPING MY GIFT

Every good and perfect gift is from above.

James 1:17

When God made me, he created me with special talents and abilities, even before I was born. His plan for my life is to use the gifts he put in me. When I think about what I want to be when I grow up, I also want to know what those special gifts are. I can ask my parents and my teachers what they think my gifts are.

When I use those gifts in ways that help others, I am doing God's will. I can enjoy serving and obeying God because I always get to use the gifts he has given me. Because God loves me, he always gives good gifts, and that makes my love for him grow.

───

Thank you, God, for all your gifts. Thank you for the wonderful way you made me. Thank you for everything you have put inside of me—my gifts and talents and abilities. I can hardly wait to see how you plan to use all these gifts when I grow up. In the meantime, I dedicate myself and all my gifts to you. Use me however you can and let me bring honor to you for the way you made me. Amen.

23

BEING HAPPY

For in him we live and move and have our being.

Acts 17:28

Is the purpose of life to be happy? No, the purpose of life is to make God happy. I make him happy when I obey him. He's most happy when I love and worship him, and thank him whether I feel happy or not. In fact, he created me so that I am truly happy only when I am pleasing him. The truest and most lasting happiness comes only when my goal is making God happy.

———————

Dear God, it's easy to be happy when things are going great. But when things aren't so great, it's really hard for me to feel happy. Help me to understand that whatever happens, and however I feel, you are with me. That's enough to make me happy. Forgive me, God, for thinking your job is to make me happy. Help me remember I'm here to serve you and not the other way around. Amen.

BEING DIFFERENT

"As the heavens are higher than the earth,
so are my ways higher than your ways and
my thoughts than your thoughts."

Isaiah 55:9

I know it is not always going to be easy to follow God. Why? Because God's way of doing things is often different from mine. There are times when I know what I should do, but other times I will need to wait before acting. I'll need to ask God what he wants me to do. That is the way he will teach me to trust him and not myself. If, in my deepest heart, I want to make God happy, he will always show me what to do.

Noah knew that God's ways aren't our ways. When Noah built the ark, his friends didn't know what he was doing. But he started drawing up plans, buying lumber, and calculating measurements. Noah's friends probably thought he was crazy. Not many folks who live in the desert need boats! Following God wasn't easy for Noah. Noah obeyed God even when it wasn't easy, and we've had rainbows ever since. Is there something you feel God is leading you to do that might not be easy? God will bless you for obeying him, even when others may not understand.

WHO LIVES INSIDE?

Jesus replied, "Very truly I tell you, no one can
see the kingdom of God unless they are born again."

John 3:3

Being born again means God puts his life (his Spirit) in
me and makes things new and fresh. When the Holy
Spirit lives inside me, God is inside me. When the Holy
Spirit lives inside of me, he will help me learn how to hear
God's voice.

I can learn to listen to the Spirit of God inside me.
I'll ask God right now to show me how to hear his voice.
Listening to the Holy Spirit will help me understand God
better and know what he wants me to do.

Dear God, I know I've done the easy part. I've asked you
to live in my heart. But I also want to learn to follow
you and grow up into the person you created me to be. I
pray that the Holy Spirit will teach me more about you
and your love for me—even if I don't always understand
what that means. Amen.

SOMEONE'S
ALWAYS WATCHING

"Let your light shine before others, that they may
see your good deeds and glorify your Father in heaven."

Matthew 5:16

Since I have the Holy Spirit in me, I will always want his
presence to affect the way I treat people. Would my
behavior this week and the way I have treated others make
people think better of God or worse? How about my family
and my friends? What would they think? Have I said or
done anything that would make them question whether the
Holy Spirit is guiding me? Would they think I am listening
to how he would want me to speak and act?

Do I need to ask anyone for forgiveness? If I have done
anything to damage God's reputation I will just confess it
and ask those I may have hurt to forgive me. Then I will
trust God to help me the next time.

— — — — —

Dear God, forgive me when I do the wrong thing. Forgive
me when I behave in a way that would make others
think less of you. Forgive me for being selfish or unkind
or resentful. Create in me a clean heart, O God. Thank
you for forgiving me. And thank you for loving me and
helping me live a life that pleases you and blesses other
people. Amen.

GOD, HELP!

In my distress I called to the LORD; I cried to my God
for help. From his temple he heard my voice;
my cry came before him, into his ears.

Psalm 18:6

S ometimes I can learn the most about growing up by
going through a difficult, uncomfortable experience.
That is because I am more likely to ask God for help when
I don't know what to do. God wants me to be dependent on
him when things are going good and when I am in trouble.
He wants me to learn that I always need him, whether I
feel like I do or not.

God, just because I can't see the sun on rainy days
doesn't mean the sun has gone away. Help me
remember that just because I can't see you working in
my life sometimes doesn't mean you aren't here with
me. Today I will trust in your love whether things are
going good or bad. Amen.

WHAT DO I SEE?

And all of us, with unveiled faces, seeing the glory
of the Lord as though reflected in a mirror,
are being transformed into the same image.

2 Corinthians 3:18 NRSV

When I look in a mirror, I see my own image. I can
learn to look at Jesus by reading about him in his
Word (the Bible) and by praying, being obedient, and
thinking about him. I can even get a picture in my mind
of him helping me and walking alongside me.

The more I learn to think about Jesus, his life, and
teachings, the more I will look like him in the way I behave
toward others. One reason Jesus came to earth was to
show me what a person talks and acts like when he is
following God's ways. Obeying God is what makes me look
like Jesus. Nothing is more important than learning to be
like Jesus.

Dear God, keeping my eyes on you would be much easier
if you were right in front of me like the TV. But I know
you've given me your words in the Bible and the Holy
Spirit is inside me. Show me how to look toward Jesus
and then help me have a desire in my deepest heart to
be like him. Amen.

FIRST PLACE

"Seek first his kingdom and his righteousness,
and all these things will be given to you as well."

Matthew 6:33

God has chosen me for the purpose of becoming like Jesus. The only way that can happen is for me to spend time with him.

Praying and thinking about him throughout the day and night are the ways I can spend time with him. Also, by taking the time to read his Word—especially the stories of Jesus in the Bible—he can reveal to me what Jesus was like and show me how he wants me to live and think.

Since Jesus is the model for my life, I never want to be so busy that I forget to spend time with him. I want to put him first and everything else in my life second.

— — — —

Jesus, I'm smart enough to figure out that there must be more to looking like you than simply wanting to be a nice person. Becoming more like you must be a combination of what I'm willing to let you do in my life and how much I'm willing to let you change me on the inside (transforming my desires). Help me put you first in my life. Amen.

EVER WONDER WHY?

And we know that in all things God works
for the good of those who love him, who have
been called according to his purpose.

Romans 8:28

God promises that he can use whatever happens to me for a purpose. The purpose he has in mind is that I would become more like his Son, Jesus.

When Jesus suffered bad things, he was able to learn from them. He knew his Father in heaven was so wise and loving that he could bring something good out of those difficult experiences. Often the bad things are the very things God uses for our good.

I want to learn to expect God to be present in every single event of my life whether it seems good or bad. I know he loves me and won't allow anything to happen to me that he can't use to make me more like Jesus.

— — — — —

God, the people in the Bible who believed in you experienced all kinds of things, both good and bad. You used both kinds of experiences to teach them to trust in you more. It's a little like when my mom bakes a cake. She uses ingredients that don't taste good by themselves, like flour, oil, and raw eggs. But when she mixes it all together and puts it in the oven . . . Yum! Help me not to react to every little thing that happens but trust you to mix it all together. You're making something beautiful out of my life. Amen.

I'M IN GOD'S HANDS

"Look at the birds of the air; they do not sow or reap
or store away in barns, and yet your heavenly Father
feeds them. Are you not much more valuable than they?"

Matthew 6:26

Jesus tells me my heavenly Father, who cares for the birds and flowers, also cares for me.

I know God will never forget about me. He never has, and he never will. Even when others let me down, God always cares about me. I'm much more valuable to God than birds and animals. If he takes care of them, he will take care of me. I need to remind myself of that every day.

— — — —

Just like Mom or Dad pays attention to the small details in my life, God pays attention to my needs. God cares about big things (like whether I have enough to eat and a warm bed in which to sleep) and little things (like bumps and bruises and things that get broken). God cares about everything. Is there something that's bothering me right now? Have I told God about it? Thank you, God, for caring about me. Amen.

PULLING WEEDS

"The cares of the world, and the lure of wealth,
and the desire for other things come in and choke
the word, and it yields nothing."

Mark 4:19 NRSV

There are a lot of things that can seem more important than my relationship with God. Things like friends, sports, and TV can push God out of my life just like weeds can choke the good things out of a garden.

Every day I want to remind myself that my relationship with God is the most important thing. Spending time with him each morning—reading his Word, and then praying and thinking about him—is a good way to do that.

I want to start every day like that.

God, I don't want you to be pushed out of my life. I confess I forget to pray, I forget to seek your guidance, and I forget to thank you for lots of things. But, God, I'm thanking you now for your love and your faithfulness. And I'm asking you now to guide my thoughts and direct my feet, that everywhere I go and everything I do pleases you. Amen.

FILL ME UP

"By myself I can do nothing."
John 5:30

The only way I can live fully for God is to be full of the Holy Spirit.

Right now I ask God to fill me with the Holy Spirit and teach me how to listen to his voice inside me. I need to learn to let the Holy Spirit lead me and guide me. Sometimes his "voice" is very soft, and I need to be quiet and listen.

The Holy Spirit in me is always pleasing to God, and he can show me how to think and act in a way that gives God pleasure. When I walk alongside the Holy Spirit and listen to his voice, I will always be my best for God.

— — — —

Dear God, I know that the Holy Spirit already lives in me, but I want him to completely fill me. Whatever that means, however you make that happen, and wherever it leads, I ask you to do it right now. Fill my heart, my mind, and my soul with your love. Amen.

GOD'S WAY IS THE BEST WAY

And God spoke to Israel in a vision at night and said,
"Jacob! Jacob!" "Here I am," he replied. "I am God,
the God of your father," he said. "Do not be afraid."

Genesis 46:2–3

I can learn to hear the voice of God.

God often speaks to me through my circumstances—
the things that happen to me and around me every day. In
fact, when something happens that bothers me, I just need
to ask, "God, are you trying to say something to me? Are
you trying to teach me something?"

I will always remember that the most important thing
is not getting my own way but letting God have his way.
When things don't go the way I want them, I can always
turn to God and pray, "Help me discover what it is you're
trying to teach me."

God, here I am. I give all of me, and all my
circumstances, good and bad, to your care and keeping.
Use every single thing that happens to me today to
teach me how much you love me. Be with me in my
coming and going. Thank you for the gift of life today.
Amen.

TWO EARS, ONE MOUTH

The LORD came and stood there, calling as at
the other times, "Samuel! Samuel!" Then Samuel said,
"Speak, for your servant is listening."

1 Samuel 3:10

I want to get into the habit of praying, "God, speak to
me," and then making time to listen. He might speak
to me through the adults in my life, through my friends,
or through things that happen throughout the day. Or he
might speak to me through something I read in the Bible,
or even in a soft "inner voice."

The thing that's important is that I am always paying
attention—I am always expecting to hear him speak. I will
never know when God wants to show me something very
special, and I want to be ready at all times.

––––––

God, I want to know you. I want to learn how to listen
to you. Keep my eyes wide open to your presence in my
life. Teach me what it means to hear your voice. I know
you love me and want to talk with me just like I talk
with you. Show me how that works. I want to hear your
voice. Amen.

MISSION ACCOMPLISHED

> I will not venture to speak of anything except
> what Christ has accomplished through me . . .
> through the power of the Spirit of God.
>
> *Romans 15:18,19*

My purpose in life is to be my best for God.
Being my best for God means learning to love like he
loves. My mission (the most important goal for me to have)
is to live in such a way that others see the love of God in
me. I want them to see it so clearly that it makes them
want to know him like I know him.

Loving the people around me and treating them in a
kind way shows others that I know God. If they see my
loving behavior, they will want to know him like I know him.

———

A long time ago a man named Saint Francis of Assisi,
who gave himself completely to God, said, "Proclaim the
gospel always, and when necessary use words." Saint
Francis must have meant that the way we live speaks
louder than our words.

FEBRUARY

IT'S NOT A SECRET

For he has rescued us from the dominion of darkness
and brought us into the kingdom of the Son he loves,
in whom we have redemption, the forgiveness of sins.

Colossians 1:13–14

The reason Jesus died on the cross was to make it possible for every person in the world to be friends with God. Jesus took all my sin to the cross when he died. When he rose from the dead, he made it possible for me to have new life as well.

Since God has forgiven all my sins and the Holy Spirit is in me, I want to live in such a way that others will also want to know him as I do.

— — — —

God, redemption is a strange-sounding word. It isn't a word I hear anywhere but church. Sounds kind of old-fashioned to me. I think redemption means I belong to you. That means I can go into this day knowing I have a good relationship with the One who created me and everything that is. God, I'm glad Jesus made everything right between us—now, today, this very minute, and every day to come, forever and always. Amen.

THE FRONT OF THE LINE

Jesus said, "Peace be with you!
As the Father has sent me, I am sending you."

John 20:21

M aking Jesus known to others is one of the most important things I can do. Because it is so important, I want to learn to put it ahead of other things—ahead of friends, hobbies, being popular, and even having the things I want.

This is my prayer: "God, I want to dedicate my whole life to telling others about Jesus. Jesus, help me live in such a way that others want to know you too. Holy Spirit, give me the words to say to others who want to get to know you."

— — — —

Dear God, how do I tell others about you and your love? Do I talk about you whether someone wants to hear about you or not? I don't think so. When you told people about God, you talked about sheep and goats and lost coins and lamps under beds and a runaway son and, well, you told stories. Help me know when and how to tell the story of your love—when to open my mouth and when to keep it closed. Amen.

EVERYBODY SHOULD KNOW

I am not ashamed of the gospel,
because it is the power of God that brings
salvation to everyone who believes.

Romans 1:16

I want to be so committed to showing others the love of Jesus that I won't let anything keep me from my mission. I won't care what others think of me or how they treat me. I just want God to use me to bring other people to him. No matter what kind of work I do or where I live, I want my life to be all about helping others get to know my best friend.

———

God, I don't always know what to say, and there's so much I don't understand. I guess the main thing I want to do is to live in a way that shows others that I know you and that I'm full of your love. If you'll help me do that, then others will ask me about you. I'll have the chance to tell them how great you are. Then they'll want to know you too. Amen.

WILLING TO GIVE IT ALL

It has always been my ambition
to preach the gospel.
Romans 15:20

The reason I can be so serious about my mission is because of how much Jesus loves me. He was willing to die for me, so I could become everything God created me to be. It only makes sense that I would be willing to live, so others could know him. Then they can be everything he created them to be too.

My goal will be to "know God and make him known to others." Then I will discover the gifts and talents God has given me to help others get to know him.

– – – – –

Today, God, is there a simple gift of your love that I can give to someone I love? A kind word to my brother or sister, a little gift, or a note to my mom or dad? Show me ways to put your love into action, God. Bring the ideas to my mind and the willingness to my feet. Amen.

FOLLOW THE LEADER

I became a servant of this gospel by the gift of God's
grace given me through the working of his power.

Ephesians 3:7

A m I willing to live my life in a way that others will
come to know God?

Living my life for God means I will want to do anything
God wants me to do. Sometimes that could be something
different from what I would like to do. Or it might even be
something difficult. Whatever it is, I know I can trust him
to help me.

When I dream about the future and what I will be
when I grow up, my prayer will be, "Lord, I will follow you
wherever you lead me. I know it might be different than
what I have in mind for myself, but that's ok. I know you
will show me your dreams for my life."

God, some people think daydreaming is a waste of
time, but in the Bible you spoke through dreams so you
must not think daydreaming is wasting time. Maybe
daydreaming is one way you can get me to sit still long
enough to hear your voice. I don't know for sure what
I want to do when I grow up, but I do have dreams and
hopes. I just want my dreams and hopes to bring me
closer to you. Amen.

100 PERCENT

We are not trying to please people but God,
who tests our hearts.

1 Thessalonians 2:4

When I give myself to God to obey him, he accepts my gift of myself. I belong to him. He can ask me to do anything he wants. That may seem a little scary, like walking into a completely dark room. But I can always be sure he will be with me.

If I'm afraid or uncertain about what God may ask me to do, I will ask him to help me. He will help me want to follow the plans he has for my life. He loves me and would never ask me to do something that isn't good for me.

Dear God, I do want to follow your leading. Help me have the desire to do your will. Help me, dear God, to want to want to. I know I can do anything you ask of me. Thank you, God, for giving me the power to do what I can't on my own. Amen.

GETTING TO KNOW GOD

> The Spirit helps us in our weakness;
> for we do not know how to pray as we ought,
> but that very Spirit intercedes with sighs
> too deep for words.
>
> *Romans 8:26 NRSV*

Praying is an important way for me to get to know God better. And I need to remember that the main reason to pray is not to get things from God, but rather to get to know God.

Prayer is just as much listening as talking. When I don't know what to say to God, I can just listen. I can also learn to let the Holy Spirit show me what is on God's heart for me.

When I watch a person speak in sign language for the deaf, I see that the person translates spoken words into signs that a deaf person can understand. That's a little bit like what the Holy Spirit does for me when I don't know how to pray. I simply tell God about my confusion and ask that the Holy Spirit would help me pray. Then my prayers always agree with the will of God.

WWJD?

Those God foreknew he also predestined
to be conformed to the image of his Son, that he might
be the firstborn among many brothers and sisters.

Romans 8:29

Here's the question: Do I really want to be set apart for God's purposes and only for God's purposes? I can choose to fill my life with many things. Not all the choices that distract me from God are bad things. But if my activities become more important than God, then I've let the wrong things become important.

I don't ever want to forget to take the time to talk to him about my day and ask him what he wants me to be and do.

— — — —

When a flashlight needs new batteries, the light is not nearly as bright as it should be. If I get too busy to spend time with God I'll end up like a flashlight that needs new batteries. I might give off a little light, but the light will be much dimmer than what God had planned. God, teach me how to "recharge" my spiritual batteries. I never want the light of your life in me to grow dim.

TOOLS

God will meet all your needs according
to the riches of his glory in Christ Jesus.

Philippians 4:19

I know that when God asks me to do something for him he gives me everything I need to do it. So, when I say, "God, I will do anything you want me to do. I will follow you wherever you want me to go," I never need to fear.

If God asks me to do something or go somewhere, he will go with me and help me do it. He will give me everything I need to follow him.

— — — —

With your help, God, I know I can do anything you ask of me. Thank you, God, for giving me the strength and wisdom to do for you what I can't do on my own. Thank you for your Word that says, "I can do all things through Christ who strengthens me" (Philippians 4:13). I know you always keep your word. Amen.

SEEING WITH DIFFERENT EYES

I keep asking that the God of our Lord Jesus Christ,
the glorious Father, may give you the Spirit of wisdom
and revelation, so that you may know him better.

Ephesians 1:17

Anything worth knowing takes time and practice. Learning to trust God for everything takes as much practice as learning anything else, maybe more. I want to learn to trust God for everything, so I will pray like this: "Lord, I will not trust myself, my own strength or my own thoughts. Help me get to know you so well that I can see things through your eyes and learn to trust you."

In school I learn a lot of things by studying facts and gathering information. In sports I learn a skill by practicing, like shooting a lot of free throws. But in God's kingdom there is a deeper way of learning. It's called "revelation," and it's when God helps me see his truth in my spirit, my "inner me." It's like my spirit has its own set of eyes and ears. I want to learn to see and hear God in my spirit. And so today I will practice by praying, "God, help me to learn to see and hear with the eyes and ears of my 'inner me.'"

A BIG GOD

"Truly I tell you, if you have faith as small
as a mustard seed, you can say to this mountain,
'Move from here to there,' and it will move.
Nothing will be impossible for you."

Matthew 17:20

The God who causes the sun to rise and set, who causes the seasons to change, and who causes rain and snow to fall is the God I pray to. If he can do all these things, I can be sure he has the power to help me do whatever he asks of me. After all, he's the God of the impossible!

— — — — —

God, are you really there? Are you really listening to my prayers? Do you really care about me? I know you're a big God and have a lot of things to take care of. Sometimes I don't feel your presence, and I just need a little reminder that you see me and care about me. Thank you. Amen.

GOD CARES

When I consider your heavens, the work of your fingers,
the moon and the stars which you have set in place,
what is mankind that you are mindful of them,
human beings that you care for them?

Psalm 8:4

T his is really important to understand: even though God
is the powerful creator of the universe, he is also my
God who loves me and cares for me. That's amazing! Since
he's so great and cares for me so much, it's important for
me to spend time getting to know him through prayer. The
most important thing to know about prayer is that there is
only one way to learn—and that's by simply doing it.

I learn to pray by practicing. It's just like learning
anything else. How simple is that!

＿＿＿＿

Thank you, God, for giving me the gift of life today.
Thank you for the sounds I hear as I awake each
morning. Thank you for warm covers on cold winter
mornings. Thank you for all I know and all I have yet to
learn. Help me, God, to have a desire to know you and to
be with you through prayer. Teach me to pray. Amen.

GOOD THINKING!

Show me your ways, LORD,
teach me your paths.

Psalm 25:4

Good friends often automatically know what each other is thinking. God knows what I am thinking. He wants us to be such good friends I begin to understand how he thinks and why he does what he does. Spending time together is how that will happen. I need to remember the real purpose of prayer is to get to know God.

––––––

God, I want to know you, but I don't want to be weird or "churchy." I just want to be a normal kid who loves you and cares about others. And I don't want to give in to the temptation to say mean things or make fun of other kids. Even when other kids say mean things and make fun of me, help me to be kind. Help me be who you created me to be—someone who loves you and loves others. Thanks, God. Amen.

KEEP ON TRUSTING

Do not hide your face from me when
I am in distress. Turn your ear to me;
when I call, answer me quickly.

Psalm 102:2

E ven though God and I are good friends, there will be times in my life when it seems my good friend is far away. I might pray, and it will seem like he isn't there. Or he might not answer in a way I can understand. At those times I can learn to keep trusting him no matter how I feel. Even though I can't see him and even though he feels far away, God is still my good friend. He always will be.

God, sometimes it feels like one of us has moved far away. Even when I don't understand the ways in which you are working in my life, thank you for always loving me. Thank you for little reminders of how good life is: the beauty of nature, good friends, and a loving family. There are so many ways you've blessed me. Thank you so much. Amen.

FAMOUS LAST WORDS

"You will receive power when the Holy Spirit comes on you; and you will be my witnesses."

Acts 1:8

S ome of the last words Jesus said to his disciples before he went to heaven were, "You will receive power when the Holy Spirit comes on you." I'm sure he would say his most important words to his best friends before his life ended on this earth. And if those were his most important words, I really want him to show me what he means by them.

Whatever that means and however that looks, I want the Holy Spirit to come on me. I know that's the only way I'll be able to be my best for God.

God, when I prayed and invited Jesus into my life, you gave me your Spirit to live inside of me. The Holy Spirit in me wants to fill me so full of the love of God that it spills over to those around me. His presence in me is what gives me the power to obey you and the ability to share your love with others. Here's my prayer today and every day, "Jesus, thank you for sending the Holy Spirit to fill me so I can show your love to everyone around me." Amen.

POWER

"Nothing will be impossible with God."
Luke 1:37 NRSV

Here's one of the greatest lessons I want to learn about following Jesus: When he asks me to do something, he will *always* give me the power to do it, even if I don't think I can.

I can do impossible things if I learn to trust in God. He will help me through seemingly impossible situations if I will learn to trust in him completely. Nothing is impossible with him!

Jesus, when I am faced with difficult circumstances or trials in my life, teach me to trust you. Help me to not just look at myself and what I can do. Teach me to think about what you and I can do together. When I think of how great you are and how special our friendship is, it doesn't seem like it's a hard thing to trust you. I know I can completely trust you because you love me so much. Amen.

SHINE, JESUS, SHINE

"Let your light shine before others, that they may
see your good deeds and glorify your Father in heaven."

Matthew 5:16

When the Holy Spirit is living in me, even the most ordinary things I do—playing, going to school, or helping at home—become very important. That is how I learn to let the life of God flow through me.

I don't have to do great big things for God; he just expects me to let his light shine through me in little everyday ways.

Dear God, I find it so easy to forget you. I forget to pray when I first wake up. Wanting to play, eat breakfast, watch TV, or get ready to go somewhere is usually what I think about first when I wake up. Forgive me, God, for losing track of how important you are. Be with me today in all my ordinary moments. No matter what I'm doing, let my light shine for you. In Jesus' name, amen.

BEING SORRY

One thing I do: Forgetting what is behind
and straining toward what is ahead, I press on.
Philippians 3:13–14

Sometimes I do something I wish I hadn't. Other times I don't do something I wish I had. Whenever I feel bad about something I've done or not done, I need to talk it over with Jesus and ask for forgiveness.

Once I ask for forgiveness, I am forgiven. Then I can forget about it and look forward to what God has for me just ahead.

--- --- ---

God, I can still feel bad about something even after
I've said, "I'm sorry." And even when I really mean it,
sometimes I still feel lousy. I know you forgive me, but,
God, could you help me feel forgiven? Sometimes I don't
know what to do with all these yucky feelings inside. So,
today, I'm just going to give them to you. Thanks, God,
for loving all of me—both the good and the bad. Amen.

DOING LITTLE THINGS

"Whoever wants to become great among you
must be your servant."

Matthew 20:26

I want to always remember that God humbled himself by coming to us as the baby Jesus. Even though Jesus was the all-powerful God, he was never too proud to do the smallest or most unimportant jobs as he grew older. He even washed his friends' feet—a servant's job.

Being my best for God means there's no job too small or unimportant for me to do.

- - - -

In the country where Jesus lived, people walked on dirty, dusty roads in sandals. Because of this, wealthy families often had a servant wash the feet of their guests when they arrived. I can't imagine my parents hiring someone to wash the feet of everyone who came to visit us. Yuck! I sure wouldn't want to do that. And yet that's exactly what Jesus did. He washed his friends' dirty, sweaty, and dusty feet—just like a servant. So when I'm cleaning the bathroom, picking up my toys and clothes, helping set the table, or whatever, I'm being like Jesus and doing the little things that please God.

WHY PRAY?

Your ways, God, are holy.
What god is as great as our God?
Psalm 77:13

S ometimes I will need to ask God what he wants me to
do. Other times it's right to just go ahead and do what
seems best. The better I get to know God, the more often
my everyday common sense decisions are his will for my life.

The more I get to know what God is like, the more
clearly I will know what to do. That's why prayer is so
important. Spending time with God in prayer is the way
I get to know how he thinks and feels. The closer I am to
him, the more clearly I will know his ways.

God, there's a lot I don't know. But I do know growing
up, both physically and spiritually, takes time.
Sometimes I'm impatient, but that's okay. I know you're
patient with me. Today, I trust in you, and I trust that
every day I'll understand you better. Amen.

PLEASING GOD

"Whoever can be trusted with very little
can also be trusted with much."

Luke 16:10

The best way to please God is to do ordinary, daily things with a strong desire to bring honor to him. The smallest duty done with a heart that wants to please God is a big deal.

Another way to say that is, "Whatever you do, do everything for the glory of God" (1 Corinthians 10:31).

———

God, being my best for you begins today. By doing ordinary, normal, everyday things with a willing heart and a desire to honor you, I give you my whole life. But I also need to give you my stubbornness, my impatience, my temper, and my grouchiness. I give you everything about me, both good and not so good, and ask you to help me behave in a way that pleases you. Amen.

GOD'S IN CONTROL

My help comes from the LORD, the Maker of heaven
and earth. He will not let your foot slip—he who
watches over you will not slumber.

Psalm 121:2–3

One thing I know is that God is working in every
circumstance for my good. He is never taken by
surprise. Whatever is going on in my life right now, even
if it is a difficult thing, doesn't need to make me impatient
or anxious.

I will soon understand that God knows about
everything. He cares about even little things that may not
seem important. If I will rely on him, he will use every
experience to teach me how to live the same way Jesus
lived—completely trusting in God.

— — — —

Dear God, waiting for you to work in my life can feel a
lot like waiting for Christmas. It can be hard, but I know
it is worth the wait. No matter what is happening in my
life, I will count on your guidance, strength, and help.
And then I can wait, knowing the God who watches over
me will not fall asleep and forget about me. There are
things going on in my life right now that trouble me.
Right now, God, I take the time to ask for your help. Now
I can be patient and wait for you to work it out. Amen.

OPINIONS

"We must obey God
rather than human beings!"

Acts 5:29

When my main purpose in life is to serve God and be my best for him, then it won't matter what other people think of me. Only his opinion will matter. I won't need to feel bad because someone laughs at me, doesn't like me, ignores me, or mistreats me.

I know God pays attention to me—and in time God will work things out.

— — — — —

God, what other kids think of me does matter—and
most of the time it matters more than I want to admit.
God, help me put you first, others second, and me third.
And God, when I let what others think about me become
too important, give me a new way of looking at myself
so I can see clearly that what really matters is what you
think of me. Amen.

LOVE LIVES INSIDE

God's love has been poured out into our hearts
through the Holy Spirit, who has been given to us.

Romans 5:5

When God puts his love into my heart, I not only love him, but I also love others. I love them, not because they love me, but because God has put his love for them in my heart. God's love is different from human love. God doesn't love me because *I'm* good. God loves me because *he's* good. And he loves me just as much when I'm bad as when I'm good. Just knowing that makes me want to love him back.

Jesus said, "Anyone who loves me will obey my teaching. My Father will love them, and we will come to them and make our home with them" (John 14:23). I can barely imagine what that means, that God lives in me and makes his home in me! That means he's with me all the time.

— — — —

Dear God, thank you for living in me! I know you can help me love others even when I don't feel very loving. Amen.

LOVE SERVES

We love because he first loved us.

1 John 4:19

When we really love someone or are really good friends, we care about whether they know Jesus or not. The best way for the people I love to know that Jesus loves them too is for them to see his love in me.

The best way for them to see that is for me to serve them and be kind to them.

- - - - -

Dear God, I love you, and I want those I love to know you too. Help me love others—with my words, my feelings, and my actions. In fact, God, help me love others with your love so they will want to love and serve you too. Amen.

CAN I TRUST MYSELF?

It is God who works in you to will
and to act in order to fulfill his good purpose.

Philippians 2:13

S ometimes I think it is too difficult to follow Jesus, and I
have a hard time obeying his Word. That's because I am
trusting in my own abilities and not relying on the power of
the Holy Spirit inside me. When that happens I need to ask
Jesus to give me strength. I need his strength to do what
I cannot do in my own strength. I need the power of the
Holy Spirit that Jesus promised.

— — — —

Dear God, teach me to trust in you and not in myself.
Do through me what I cannot do by myself. Jesus, be
my strength. I give you permission to make me what you
want me to be. Strengthen me on the inside, so I can
please you from my heart. Amen.

GOD ALWAYS ANSWERS

The Spirit that God has given us
does not make us timid; instead,
his Spirit fills us with power, love, and self-control.

2 Timothy 1:7 GNB

There is a reason that sometimes I feel weak and unable to be the kind of person God wants me to be. When I am trusting myself instead of turning to Jesus and asking for his help, I lose my sense of his strength and power. Prayer is what can make the difference.

Here's a prayer I know God will always answer: "Jesus, fill me with the Holy Spirit and help me live like you want me to live. Amen."

Dear God, teach me the difference between trusting in my own strength and trusting in the power of the Holy Spirit within me. Show me how to do things together with you instead of relying only on my own abilities. Help me be able to imagine the reality that you live in me and can help me in everything I do. Thank you. Amen.

LOVING JESUS

"If you love me, keep my commands."
John 14:15

I don't obey Jesus just because I have to. Jesus doesn't force me to obey him. Rather, Jesus loves me even before I do anything, say anything, or pray anything. I love Jesus because Jesus first loved me. That's why I want to do what he says. It's all about love—his love *for* me creates love *in* me for myself and others.

———

Dear God, I know you love me, but sometimes I find it hard to love myself. Sometimes I find it even harder to love others, especially _____ (think of someone, but don't write their name). Help me accept your love for me. Make your love real to me in ways I can see and feel. In asking that your love change me, I also ask you to give _____ (think of the same person as above) lots of laughter and hugs and anything else I would want for myself. Thank you, Jesus, for loving me and for loving those I have a hard time loving. Amen.

TELL GOD

"Ask and it will be given to you; seek and you will find;
knock and the door will be opened to you."

Matthew 7:7

Jesus once asked a blind man what he wanted him to do
for him. Of course, the man wanted his eyesight. That's
what was most important to him.

Jesus wants to give me my deepest desires, too.
Whenever I pray, I am talking to an all-powerful God who
is asking me to bring my dreams, my hopes, and my heart's
desires to him.

God, I know your answers may not always be the
answers I want, but they will always be the answers I
need. But knowing that doesn't make it any easier to
be patient or grateful or faithful to you. You know, God,
how much I want what I want when I want it. Change
my "wants" God. Give me your dreams for my life. Hold
me close in your care and keeping. Amen.

MARCH

SAY, "YES!"

I have hidden your word in my heart
that I might not sin against you.

Psalm 119:11

I want my love for God to be more than just a good feeling. If I say I love God and that I want to obey him, that's only the beginning. I also need to learn how God wants me to live by practicing what I read in his Word, the Bible.

The Holy Spirit who lives in me will teach me what his words mean and how to obey them.

－－－－

Dear God, show me how to hide your Word in my heart. Teach me what it means to let the light of your Word shine on the path of my life. Show me what to do, where to go, and what to say. Guide me with a sense of your presence throughout this day. Amen.

#1

Let the words of my mouth
and the meditation of my heart be acceptable
to you, O Lord, my rock and my redeemer.

Psalm 19:14 NRSV

J esus knows my heart, my thoughts, and my feelings. I have no secrets from God. I never need to try to hide anything from God because his love for me does not depend on my behavior. When I think about that, it makes me want to obey him.

I'll trust the Holy Spirit in me to help me learn to love Jesus more than anyone or anything else. Then I will always be pleasing to him.

— — — —

Jesus, sometimes I'm not sure I really know what it means to love you. I don't love you the way I love my mom or my dad. They are right here and give me hugs and take care of me. But I want to love you, and I want to know what loving you means. Thank you, Jesus, for my family, my friends, my church, and all the ways I'm able to learn about you. Amen.

REAL LOVE

"The Son of Man did not come to be served,
but to serve, and to give his life
as a ransom for many."

Matthew 20:28

I f the Holy Spirit is helping me learn to love others like Jesus did, that means I will serve others like Jesus did. Just like he gave himself for me, I want to give my life to help others. That's what real love is.

— — — —

Jesus knew we would get tired. Jesus got tired and went off by himself to talk with his Father; after all, he was not only God, but he was also a human just like me. He learned how to live by the power of the Holy Spirit. When I get tired and still have to go to school the next day or do chores around the house, I don't have to rely on my own strength. I can simply pray: "God, I'm tired and don't want to do what I have to do today. You're inside of me. Be my strength today. Help me be faithful to you and do what I need to do. Thank you."

I'M NOT TOO YOUNG

Your word is a lamp for my feet,
a light on my path.

Psalm 119:105

E ven at my young age, I can begin to ask God to show me a clear path for my life. His Word can be like a light that shows me where to walk. Following the path he shows me makes him very happy. I always want to remember: I am not my own. I belong to him. I want my feet to walk in his path. I want his Word to light my way.

– – – – –

Where my feet take me says a lot about my life. When I think back over yesterday, I realize my feet took me to the places most important to me. When I pray that God's Word would be a lamp to my feet and light for my path, I am just asking him to show me where to go and to be in charge of everything I do and everywhere I go. I want to walk in his light no matter what. Amen.

BEST FRIENDS

I have called you by name,
you are mine.
Isaiah 43:1 NRSV

God created me, so he could have a loving friendship with me. The better I understand that incredible truth, the more clearly I will understand what he wants me to do with my life. The closer I am to him, the easier it will be to hear his voice—to know how he feels about me in his heart. When I know how he feels about me in his heart, I will want to love, worship, and obey him.

———

God, have you really called me by name? It seems hard to believe that you, the One who created heaven and earth, could actually know me by name? How can you possibly know me when there are so many people in the world? But the Bible says that not only do you know me but you are also with me all the time. God, that's awesome! Help me to always remember that's true, whether I feel like it or not. Amen.

FEELINGS

"Be strong and courageous. Do not be afraid or terrified
because of them, for the LORD your God goes with you;
he will never leave you nor forsake you."

Deuteronomy 31:6

Sometimes I don't feel like God is very close or very
"friendly." I want to learn that I cannot trust the way
I feel, but I can always trust God's Word. God's Word says
that he will never leave me. That's the truth, and I believe
it, no matter how I feel! I am never alone!

— — — — —

Dear Jesus, I am afraid at times. Help me learn how to
give my fears to you, trusting that your love is bigger
than my fear. You always keep your word. I never need
to fear because you're with me. Amen.

NOTHING LIKE GOD'S LOVE

For I am convinced that neither death nor life,
neither angels nor demons, neither the present nor
the future, nor any powers, neither height nor depth,
nor anything else in all creation, will be able to separate
us from the love of God that is in Christ Jesus our Lord.

Romans 8:38

God loves me, not because I'm such a great person but because he is so good at loving. There is nothing I can do to earn God's love. He just loves me. And there is nothing I can do to make him not love me. God is never unloving! He will always love me, no matter what! That's who he is!

- - - -

God, today I ask for a grateful heart. Your love is a gift I can too easily take for granted—and I don't want to do that. A lot of yucky things can happen and sometimes do happen. Friends ignore me and hurt my feelings. People I love go away or get sick. I forget to do my homework or get into trouble. God, help me remember that even when yucky things happen, your love is always with me. Amen.

GIVE EVERYTHING

I urge you, brothers and sisters, in view of God's mercy,
to offer your bodies as a living sacrifice, holy and
pleasing to God—this is your true and proper worship.

Romans 12:1

W hen I decide to follow Jesus, he asks me to offer him
the bad things about me (my sins, so he can take
them away). But he also wants me to give him the good
things about me (my talents and abilities). If I will give him
everything, he will help make the bad things get weaker
and make the good things better.

A long time ago a young man loved to run and dreamed
of running in the Olympics. He felt closer to God when
running than at any other time. He realized if he offered
his body as a "living sacrifice" to God, he could serve
God by running in the Olympics. The young man won
the Olympic gold medal in 1924. Eric Liddel, known
as the "Flying Scotsman," presented his body to God
and served God by doing what he loved most. Is there
something I love doing that I could "give back" to God
as a "living sacrifice"? Do I love art, sports, music, or
school work? Anything I love to do I want to do as a
"living sacrifice" to God.

NO TURNING BACK

"You do not want to leave too, do you?" Jesus asked the
Twelve. Simon Peter answered him, "Lord, to whom
shall we go? You have the words of eternal life."

John 6:67–68

E ven though I am really young, I have made up my
mind: I'm going to follow Jesus the rest of my life.
I know it will not always be easy. But, no matter what
happens, I can trust him because he loves me. I'm never
turning back!

I may not always know what will happen next, but
I know that God knows and that he cares. God has the
power to make everything turn out just the right way,
so I will trust him.

Dear God, I'm all yours! Keep me close to you, and let
me walk in your ways, not only this day but every day.
Amen.

I'M GOD'S CHILD

Dear friends, now we are children of God,
and what we will be has not yet been made known.
But we know that when Christ appears,
we shall be like him, for we shall see him as he is.

1 John 3:2

I am a child of God.

Children are usually like their parents in many ways.
God's purpose for me is to help me love like he loves.
That means letting the love of God become more and
more real to me so my actions, my thoughts, my choices—
everything—are shaped by his love.

The Holy Spirit helps me look like my heavenly Father
by the way I love others.

– – – – –

Dear God, make of me whatever you want me to be.
Sometimes I like being me, and sometimes I don't.
Sometimes I like my life, and sometimes I don't. But no
matter whether I'm having a good day or a not-so-good
day, be the Lord of all my thoughts and feelings. Amen.

WAIT

If we hope for what we do not yet have,
we wait for it patiently.

Romans 8:25

As I grow up in my Christian life, there will be times when I know very clearly what God wants me to do. At other times, it will not be very easy to know.

During the times I don't know what to do, God wants to teach me how to be patient and wait on him. Waiting times are when God is working inside me by his Spirit to make me more like Jesus.

Jesus, I've never really liked waiting. I don't like waiting in line to get ice cream. I don't like waiting at the dentist's office. And I don't like waiting for the sun to come back after it rains for a long time. But waiting is a big part of life. Help me see that you're always working in my life even when it seems like I'm just waiting around and nothing's happening. So even when I don't like to wait, help me trust that you are at work in my life. Amen.

SOMETHING BETTER

"Love the LORD your God with all your heart
and with all your soul and with all your mind
and with all your strength."

Mark 12:30

Following Jesus is sometimes easy and joyful, but at other times it is difficult and confusing. Things I want will seem very important, and sometimes I will want to go my own way instead of God's way.

Following Jesus may mean putting aside what I want, so God can replace it with something much better. Just like a good parent, he loves me too much to always give me exactly what I want.

God, the verse today says you want me to give you my feelings (heart), my brain (mind), my body (strength), and even my whole personality (soul). So, God, I give all of me to all of you. Here is my heart, soul, mind, and body. Forgive me, God, when I hold anything back from you. I want you to have all of me. Amen.

BEING MY BEST

"God so loved the world that he gave his
one and only Son, that whoever believes in him
shall not perish but have eternal life."

John 3:16

"**G**od so loved the world that he gave . . ."
A person who loves is a person who loves to give.
God first loved me and gave me the gift of Jesus, so I
could know what God was truly like. I want to learn to be
a "giver" like my heavenly Father. I want to learn to think
more about others and less about me and how everything
affects me.

I want to be so in love with God that I don't think twice
about giving him everything I am and have.

Lord, I give you all of me—my wants, desires, and plans.
Help me become exactly what you want me to be. I just
want to be my best for you. Amen.

PERFECT WAY TO START THE DAY

Whatever you do, whether in word or deed,
do it all in the name of the Lord Jesus,
giving thanks to God the Father through him.

Colossians 3:17

I don't usually see immediate results from giving myself to God. But that's okay. God's Word is like a seed planted inside me. There might not be any visible sign of life for a while, but a lot is happening underground.

Just because there isn't an immediate, visible change doesn't mean the Holy Spirit isn't working inside me. I give myself to God every day, and something incredible is happening—even though I can't always see it.

— — — —

Lord, today I give myself to you. Today and every day I will pray: Be in charge of my whole life today—my time, my words, my actions, my feelings—everything! Amen.

IT'S NOT ALWAYS EASY

Keep your eyes on Jesus, our leader and instructor.
He was willing to die a shameful death on the cross
because of the joy he knew would be his afterwards.

Hebrews 12:2 TLB

Sometimes I will enjoy following Jesus, and sometimes I won't. A friend might make fun of me, something bad might happen, or something I really want to happen won't.

When I am sad or confused, I will remember Jesus. It wasn't always easy for him either, yet he knew his heavenly Father was with him. Although it's hard to enjoy bad experiences, they can help me learn to trust God more.

Jesus died on the cross—the worst possible thing that could happen to any human being. But that wasn't the end of the story. The end of the story was Jesus rising from the dead. No matter what happens in the story of my life, God can use it to bring me new life. He can make me better than I was before it happened to me.

CONFESS QUICKLY

If we confess our sins, he is faithful and just
and will forgive us our sins and purify us
from all unrighteousness.

1 John 1:9

Confession has three parts: telling God what I did wrong, admitting that I'm sorry I did it, and asking him to forgive me. A fourth part might be apologizing to someone who was hurt by what I did wrong.

I won't wait to confess my sins. I'll do it right away. It is much harder to do it later. Besides, I don't want anything to come between me and God or between me and another person.

Everyone is a sinner. Everyone does things that shouldn't be done. Everyone! There are no exceptions. Me included! My sin hurts my relationship with God. I need to be forgiven so there's nothing coming between me and my best friend. God loves me too much to want anything to come between us.

— — — —

God, help me see what I need to confess, so I don't let sin separate me from your love. Amen.

WINNERS AND LOSERS

I consider everything a loss because
of the surpassing worth of knowing
Christ Jesus my Lord.

Philippians 3:8

S uccess, money, fame, popularity, and happiness—
nothing even comes close to the joy of knowing Jesus
and following his ways. If I focus on knowing him and make
it my aim to please him, I will be blessed with everything I
need. I will be happy no matter what my life looks like.

— — — —

Dear God, there are so many things I want—and my list
seems to change every day. When it comes to making
wish lists and Christmas lists and birthday lists, I'm
a pro. My "I wants" could fill a book. But more than
any of that, I want to live my life for you. God, change
my "wants" to be all the things you want for me. While
you're at it, God, could you give me what it takes to trust
that what you want for me is what's best? Amen.

WASHING UP

He saved us through the washing of rebirth
and renewal by the Holy Spirit, whom he poured out
on us generously through Jesus Christ our Savior.

Titus 3:5–6

Just as it is important to wash my body every day, it is
even more important to keep clean spiritually. I keep my
spirit clean by confessing my sin and being forgiven.

I can't make myself be good or always loving and kind.
Only God can do that. But what I can do is cooperate with
God. I can open the door of my heart and mind and let God
in, or I can keep the door closed. That choice is up to me.
If I ask him, the Holy Spirit will not only wash me clean, but
he will also make me like new again—like I had never sinned.

God, I know I can be stubborn and crabby and difficult
at times. Sometimes my mouth gets me into trouble.
God, I'm not sure what I can do to cooperate with you,
but guide me. Help me open the door of my heart and
mind to let you in, today and every day. Amen.

HAVE FAITH

To have faith is to be sure of the things we hope for,
to be certain of the things we cannot see.

Hebrews 11:1 GNB

I want to learn what it means to have faith in God. I know that faith means trusting God when I don't understand him. Faith also means that even though I don't know what's going to happen in the future, I know God knows and that I can always trust him. Lord, teach me how to have faith.

— — — — —

God, I give you my life today. I give you my future. And, by your grace, I want to give you everything in between. Thank you for teaching me that I can have faith in you. Amen.

GOOD FOR ME

"I know the plans I have for you," declares the Lord,
"plans to prosper you and not to harm you,
plans to give you hope and a future."

Jeremiah 29:11

God's Word tells me he is interested in my well-being. True friends always want what's best for each other.

God is my friend, and his desire for me is always for my good. Do I want to be my best for God? I can only give God my best if I know him. The better I get to know my heavenly Father, the more I will want to please him. And pleasing him means I'll be doing the things that are also the best for me.

— — — — —

God, sometimes I think I know you and other times I just feel confused. Help me, God, to know you as my heavenly Father. Fill my heart with unfailing trust and my mind with a desire for the truth about you. Shape my soul while I'm young, so I will know how to please you for the rest of my life. Amen.

MY WAY? NO WAY!

God is our refuge and strength,
an ever-present help in trouble.

Psalm 46:1

It is very important that I don't let anything keep me from being my best for God.

Often I will want my own way so strongly that God cannot have his way with my life. When that happens, I only need to say "I'm sorry," turn toward God and his will, and obey. That can be a hard thing to do. Jesus called the Holy Spirit "the Helper." He is there to help the moment I say, "Holy Spirit, I need your help!"

— — — — —

Lord, help me always to choose what you want instead of demanding to get my own way. Help me be willing to obey you, even when I don't feel like obeying. Change my heart, so I want what you want for me. Amen.

ONE THING
NEVER CHANGES

Jesus Christ is the same yesterday
and today and forever.

Hebrews 13:8

F eelings and emotions come and go. One day I feel very
close to God; at other times, he seems very far away.
Every day I am learning to trust God and his Word and not
my feelings and emotions.

God never changes. Jesus is always the same. He is
always near to me, whether I feel his presence or not.

- - - - -

God, knowing you are always near and feeling your
presence are two very different things. When I awake
in the middle of the night, I know there's nothing to
be afraid of. But I feel the fear anyway! Feeling afraid
and knowing the truth are two different things. Help
me, God, to accept my emotions as a gift, not a guide,
trusting in your truth no matter how I feel. Amen.

TURN ON THE LIGHT

Nothing in all creation
is hidden from God's sight.

Hebrews 4:13

When I am in a dark room everything is hidden, but as soon as I turn on the light, I can see everything!

God wants me to live in the light. By living in the light of God's love, he can show me the hidden things in my life that keep me from being my best for him. Confessing my sins and failures is how I live in the light.

I will always be honest with God. He can see in the dark anyway.

God, like sunlight coming into my window in the morning, bring the light of your loving presence into my world. Keep my eyes open. By your grace, help me see myself honestly and please bring your light to any dark emotions—anger, resentment, or jealousy—that try to take hold of my heart today. Amen.

TOUGH STUFF

During the days of Jesus' life on earth . . .
he learned obedience from what he suffered.

Hebrews 5:7–8

A t times God may allow me to go through a very
difficult situation. Tough times are not to hurt me but
to teach me to turn to God and cry, "Help!" When I feel the
most helpless and needy, that's when God is the nearest.
No matter how hard things can get, God will always be
right there with me to help me get through it. I can always
count on him.

Sometimes I feel lost and unsure and things aren't
making any sense. I feel like I'm walking in the dark.
But if I can hang in there and let God be God, he will
lead me out of the darkness and things will be better
than they were before. Thank you, God, that you can see
in the dark. I'm going to stick with you whether I can
see or not! Amen.

HOLY MEANS HAPPY

> Be made new in the attitude of your minds . . .
> put on the new self, created to be like God
> in true righteousness and holiness.
>
> *Ephesians 4:22–24*

The reason God wants me to be holy is not so people will say, "My, what a fine boy or girl that is." God wants people to see my good actions and attitudes and say, "Wow! Isn't God great! Look what God has made of that child."

God, let my actions honor you, let my thoughts be lined up with your thoughts about me, and let my heart be filled with your love. Let all I do please you. Amen.

A CLEAR VIEW

"Blessed are the pure in heart,
for they will see God."

Matthew 5:8

Pure water has no specks or dirt in it. Pure gold shines brightly. Fresh-fallen snow is pure white.

God wants me to be pure—free of any speck or blemish of sin. When I am pure in heart, people can look right through me and see God.

God, you're the only one who can make me pure. My choices and actions can affect it a little, but only you can change me from the inside out. Make me pure in heart. Change me from the inside out. Amen.

WALK BEFORE RUNNING

To him who is able to keep you from stumbling . . .
to the only God our Savior be glory, majesty,
power and authority, through Jesus Christ our Lord,
before all ages, now and forevermore! Amen.

Jude 1:24–25

When I was learning to walk, I stumbled and fell, over and over. Growing and learning to walk spiritually is a natural part of being a follower of Jesus. If I stumble and fall when trying to follow Jesus, I'll not give up, but I'll get up! I'll just get up and start walking again. Before I know it, I'll even be running.

– – – – –

God, help me when I fall. Forgive me when I fail. And forgive me when I forget that I don't have to be perfect. Help me know you're never mad at me when I fall; instead, you're cheering me on saying, "C'mon, get up. I know you can do it!" Thank you, God, for believing in me. Amen.

KNOWING GOD BETTER

I keep asking that the God of our Lord Jesus Christ,
the glorious Father, may give you the Spirit of wisdom
and revelation, so that you may know him better.

Ephesians 1:17

Faith is knowing in my heart that I can trust God
because I know what he is like. The better I know him,
the easier it is to obey him. God, who knows me the best—
all the good and the bad—loves me the most.

- - - - -

God, one minute I'm kind and caring; the next I'm
crabby and impatient. Help me know you love me
even in my crabby moments just as much as you love
me when I'm being my best. Take the best and worst
of me and shape me into a person of great faith. Help
me become someone who knows how to trust you in
everything. Amen.

GIVE THANKS

Rejoice always, pray continually,
give thanks in all circumstances;
for this is God's will for you in Christ Jesus.

1 Thessalonians 5:16–18

I want to be careful not to get so busy with activities and things that I forget about Jesus. A good way to keep him in my thoughts is to remember all day long to thank him. I can just whisper short prayers throughout the day. I might just pray: "Thank you for this!" or "You're so great, God!" or "Wow, God, this is so beautiful!"

———

Thank you, God, for this sunrise; thank you for that friend, for my parents, for my teacher, for this good food, and for that beautiful sunset. Help me to learn to let everything and everybody remind me of you. That's the best way to feel your presence with me all day long. Amen.

GOD KNOWS

"This, then, is how you should pray."

Matthew 6:9

Prayer is not just telling God what I want. Prayer is getting to know God. God knows what I want even before I ask for anything.

The purpose of prayer isn't to get God to do things for me but to know God. Prayer is how I continually let God be at work in my life. It's like having a conversation with a best friend. The more we talk with each other, the better we get to know one another.

— — — —

God, the hard thing about prayer is that so much of the time it feels so one-sided. I do the talking, and you do the listening. I really want to let prayer be a two-way deal—you know, friends just hanging out together talking. I know you "speak" to those who love you, but, God, could you "speak" to me a little louder or a little plainer? Teach me how to listen. Amen.

PRAY FOR OTHERS

Confess your sins to each other
and pray for each other.

James 5:16

When I see something in another person that bothers me, I won't want to criticize them, laugh at them, or judge them. Those kinds of things can just be God's way of reminding me to pray for them.

I can let those things remind me of how much God loves that person and wants the best for them. So I will pray for them.

––––––

Jesus, help me to see _____ (think of someone, but don't write their name) the way you see them and help them to know how much you love them. Amen.

APRIL

WHY WORRY?

Cast all your anxiety on him
because he cares for you.

1 Peter 5:7

A m I worried about something in my family, at school, or with a friend? Prayer is how I give my worries to God, so I don't have to worry anymore. I can thank God right now for caring for me. I can give him whatever I'm worried about and then quit worrying.

God has it all under control. Why worry when I can pray?

— — — — —

God, I wish worry were like a light switch, something I could flip on or off whenever I wanted. Maybe worry is the light switch that goes on telling me when I need to pray, like a warning light or smoke alarm. Help me, God, to turn the worry off by turning to you. Help me learn to trust that all will be well no matter what happens. Amen.

WHAT'S GOD LIKE?

"I [Jesus] and the Father are one."
John 10:30

There is nothing more important than knowing Jesus. He is my picture of what God is like: knowing Jesus is how I get to know God. Jesus said if we have seen him then we have seen the Father. When I read about Jesus in the Bible, the Holy Spirit will show me what my heavenly Father is like. It's like this: the Holy Spirit shows me what Jesus is like, and then Jesus shows me what my heavenly Father is like.

––––––

When I read a favorite book or watch a favorite movie over and over again, I get to know the characters really well. I've even dressed up like some of them. I've tried to act like them and repeat some of their lines! The more I read about Jesus in the Bible, the more I will learn how he acted and talked. That's why it's so important to read the Bible—to learn everything I can about the One I want to be like.

BACK TO THE FUTURE

Forgetting what is behind and straining
toward what is ahead, I press on toward the goal
to win the prize for which God has called me
heavenward in Christ Jesus.

Philippians 3:13–14

Jesus doesn't want something bad I did in the past to make me feel bad in the present. When I sin, I ask God to forgive me. If I hurt someone else, I need to go to that person and ask him or her to forgive me. Confessing my sins and being forgiven are like taking roadblocks out of the path to the wonderful future God has for me.

———

Roadblocks make traffic go a different way, block off certain lanes, indicate a detour, or close a road. Roadblocks mean it's going to take longer to get where we want to go. God knows where he wants us to go with our lives, even when we don't. And God doesn't want us to have to take any unnecessary detours. The closer we stay to God, the fewer roadblocks we'll have.

LORD OF ALL

We take captive every thought
to make it obedient to Christ.

Corinthians 10:5

Is Jesus the Lord of my whole life? Am I prepared to let Jesus do anything with my life? Is there any part of my life that I'd rather have Jesus stay away from? Anything I'm holding back? I want to be his in every area of my life. No exceptions!

A great missionary, Jim Elliot, said, "He is no fool who gives what he cannot keep to gain what he cannot lose." I don't want to hold on to anything God wants me to let go of. I want to be free of anything holding me back from being my best for him.

I want to give my whole life to you, Jesus, no matter what it costs. I don't want to hold anything back. I make you Lord of my whole life. Show me how to let you be in charge of everything I say, do, think, and feel. Thank you for being the Lord of my life. Amen.

ONE WAY

For it was by God's own decision that the Son
has in himself the full nature of God. Through the Son,
then, God decided to bring the whole
universe back to himself.

Colossians 1:19–20 GNB

When Jesus died on a cross, he opened up the way for me to get to God. My sins kept me from a close friendship with God. On the cross Jesus said, "Give me your sins. Let me take them from you so you can be in my Father's holy presence."

In Jesus, nothing can separate me from God. Everything he did on the cross is so I can enjoy being God's close friend.

Today, everywhere I go, I'll let this thought go with me: "I am a child of God, precious in his sight. I am a child of God, precious in his sight. I am a child of God, precious in his sight."

SO MUCH MORE

"God so loved the world that he gave his
one and only Son, that whoever believes in him
shall not perish but have eternal life."

John 3:16

It's incredible to know how much God loves me. He is not only King of Kings and Lord of Lords, but he is also the Lover of Lovers. Nobody loves like he loves. He loves me so much that he sent his only Son, Jesus, to die for me on a cross. The reason it is so easy for me to come to God is because of the price Jesus paid.

***

Dear God, do you really love me that much? How can I matter to the God of the universe? But you sent your Son, Jesus, so that I could know you love me. Even though it's sometimes hard to believe you could love me that much, thank you. Thank you for a love that's bigger than my understanding. Help me grow into the love you have for me. Amen.

SOMEONE TO TEACH ME

"When he, the Spirit of truth, comes,
he will guide you into all the truth."
John 16:13

There is only one way to truly understand God's Word, the Bible. The Holy Spirit, who lives in me, will show me what it means.

Before I read the Bible I can pray, "Holy Spirit, help me understand this." One of the main reasons God sent the Holy Spirit was to help me understand who Jesus is and what he did for me. I will gain that understanding by reading about Jesus and thinking about his life. A prayer that God loves to answer is, "Holy Spirit, show me what Jesus is like; Jesus, show me what God is like."

Reading the Bible without help is like trying to read a college textbook before finishing grade school—I wouldn't understand it. I would need help from parents, teachers, and older people. God sent the best teacher of all to help me understand his Word, the Holy Spirit. Of course, I still need teachers and pastors to help me. But even at my age, I can be learning to trust the Holy Spirit to guide me and give me understanding beyond my years.

BORN TWICE

"Very truly I tell you, no one can see
the kingdom of God unless they are born again."

John 3:3

Jesus says I need to be "born again." To be born again means the Holy Spirit comes into me and gives life to that unseen part of me that can know God—my spirit, or my "inner me." My spirit will live forever with God because God is forever.

My mother gave birth to me physically. But I was born again spiritually when I invited Jesus to come into my heart. That means I have the life of God—the Holy Spirit—living inside of me.

To my spirit, prayer is food and obedience is exercise. The more I do those things, the stronger my inner life becomes. I may be young and small physically, but the life I have inside can be big and strong.

Lord, teach me how to grow in you. Amen.

KNOWING JESUS PERSONALLY

"When the Helper comes, whom I will send to you
from the Father, that is the Spirit of truth who proceeds
from the Father, He will testify about Me."

John 15:26 NASB

There is a big difference between knowing *about* Jesus and really knowing him. I could know all about someone famous by reading books and checking out websites, but that doesn't mean I really know them as a close friend.

I can read about Jesus in the Bible, but I want to do more than know about him. The Holy Spirit helps me get to know him more deeply—like a close friend. Friends really *know* each other, not just *about* each other. Jesus wants to be that kind of friend.

Jesus, help me to know you and not just know about you.
As I read the book about you—the Bible—I ask that the
Holy Spirit would teach me who Jesus really is. More
than anything, I want to know him. I want to be like
him. Holy Spirit, reveal Jesus to me. Amen.

SAY "NO" TO SIN!

Cleanse me from my sin . . .
Wash me, and I will be whiter than snow.

Psalm 51:2–7

I f I want Jesus to be my Lord, I will want to decide to always tell God as soon as I know I have sinned. Sin always affects my relationship with God and my ability to sense his presence.

Because he loves me no matter what, I never need to be afraid to tell God about what I've done. The sooner I confess, the better my relationship with him will be. Is there anything I need to tell God about right now?

— — — —

Jesus, I don't want anything to come between me and you. If there is anything I feel bad about or uncomfortable about, help me see if there's something I need to confess. I just want to be completely honest with you. Help me. Amen.

FATHER AND CHILD

Because you are children, God has sent the Spirit
of his Son into our hearts, crying, "Abba Father!"

Galatians 4:6 NRSV

God's plan for me is that I would have a father/child relationship with him just like Jesus did. The Holy Spirit in me is the one who gives me the ability to have this close, personal relationship with God. Learning to hear and obey all the Holy Spirit shows me is how I will grow deeper in my friendship with God.

God, I know you want to be as close to me as the air I breathe and the people I hug. So, could you make knowing you a little bit easier, even if just for today? Amen.

ETERNAL MEANS FOREVER

Let us hold fast to the confession
of our hope without wavering,
for he who has promised is faithful.

Hebrews 10:23 NRSV

Eternal life is the gift of God. Eternal life means that not only can I enjoy the presence of God in the here and now but that I will also live forever with God.

When God put his Spirit into me, I was born again, and now I have eternal life. When my body dies, I will go to be with God in a much better world than I've ever imagined. But in the meantime, right now, in this life, the Holy Spirit helps me enjoy a generous sample of what it will be like to live in God's presence in heaven. You could call that "heaven on earth!"

God, thank you for your gift of eternal life. What seems so great is that I can experience a lot of the good things about that future life right now—the joy, peace, and love I will know when I am with you in heaven. The Holy Spirit can produce all those things in me while I'm still on this earth. I don't have to wait to experience eternal life. It begins right here and now! Amen.

JESUS IS
HERE TO HELP

"Come to me, all you who are weary and burdened,
and I will give you rest."

Matthew 11:28

Sometimes a situation causes me to worry. When I'm
worried, tired, or overwhelmed, God wants to help
carry the weight of my troubles. When Jesus is helping me
carry a heavy burden, he is the closest to me. I don't need
to get frustrated! I just need to learn to enjoy his presence.

———

Jesus, I don't want my worry to crowd out your love.
Help me learn that when things are the most difficult
for me, you are the closest to me. Help me feel your
presence most when things are the hardest for me.
Amen.

WHAT, ME WORRY?

Do not worry about anything, but in everything
by prayer and supplication with thanksgiving
let your requests be made known to God.

Philippians 4:6 NRSV

There is no problem too big for God! I can learn to thank God for everything—even problems. God allows problems into my life, so I will turn to him and ask for his help and friendship. Facing problems together is what good friends do. That's when I can enjoy God's friendship the most. Next time I have a problem, I think I'll shout out, "I love problems!" Then I'll just relax and work with God to solve it.

— — — —

God, sometimes problems do seem bigger than you. Sometimes I wish you would act in a bigger, more obvious way. Just trusting feels like doing nothing. But, God, even when I feel this way, I still know that you and I can face my problems together. I know you want the best for me, so I'm going to trust you, problems or no problems. Amen.

NEVER FORGET
TO EXERCISE

Train yourself to be godly.
For physical training is of some value,
but godliness has value for all things,
holding promise for both the present life
and the life to come.

1 Timothy 4:7–8

Being a follower of Jesus takes discipline. My spirit needs exercise just like my body. There are three exercises I will want to do regularly in order to stay spiritually fit:

- Read God's Word, the Bible, and ask the Holy Spirit for understanding.

- Pray and learn to listen to God.

- Keep friendships with others who are also followers of Jesus.

For hundreds of years, followers of Jesus have practiced spiritual disciplines like these. Disciplines are practices that will strengthen my relationship with God. If I lift weights in the gym, my muscles will get bigger and stronger. Disciplines are like lifting "spiritual weights." Through these exercises my spirit (my inner person) gets stronger, and I am better able to live a life that is pleasing to God.

COUNT ON GOD

The LORD is my protector;
he is my strong fortress. My God is my protection,
and with him I am safe. He protects me like a shield;
he defends me and keeps me safe.

Psalm 18:2 GNB

Feelings come and go. Feelings have nothing to do with how close God is to me, how much he loves me, or how deeply he cares about everything going on in my life.

God never changes. He is always true to who he is. I can always count on him no matter how I feel.

God, when I read the words "feelings come and go," I can't help but think how easy that sounds, but how tough it is to practice. If I could have it my way, I'd rather keep the good feelings and do away with the bad. But since life doesn't seem to work that way, I'll try to take each day as it comes, trusting that bad days—and bad feelings—won't last forever. Amen.

JUST DO IT!

Give me an eagerness for your laws
rather than a love for money!

Psalm 119:36 NLT

If I wait until I *feel* like spending time with God—reading the Bible, praying and listening—I may never get around to doing it. But once I start doing it, the feeling will most likely follow.

Growing in my relationship with God requires discipline. I need to teach myself to do what needs to be done, whether I feel like doing it or not. I always want to be eager to know God and do what pleases him.

— — — —

Jesus, when I think you are asking me to do something, help me to respond quickly and willingly. I don't want to wait, stall, think, or hesitate. Help me, God, to just do it, in your name. Teach me how to live a disciplined life. Amen.

NO JOB TOO SMALL

Whatever you do, work at it with all your heart,
as working for the Lord,
not for human masters . . .

Colossians 3:23

I want to be willing to do whatever I am asked to do, no
matter how big or small it seems. The important thing isn't
the size of the task; the important thing is that I do it with a
sense that Jesus is with me and my doing it honors him.

If he is doing it with me and my heart wants to please
him, no job is a small job. Everything is important.

Jesus, today I ask that in everything I do, I will bring
honor to you. Let no job—not even picking up my
clothes or straightening up my bedroom—be too small
for me to do for you. Amen.

STAYING CLOSE TO MY FRIEND

"And lead us not into temptation,
but deliver us from the evil one."

Matthew 6:13

A temptation is anything that draws me away from my friendship with God. A temptation might even be something good that distracts me from God's best. It could be something as simple as a TV show, playing video games, or a sleepover at a friend's house.

If it comes between me and God, I want to resist it. And when I resist it, I become more patient and stronger in my faith.

God, give me strength to turn away from anything, good or bad, that gets in the way of my friendship with you. Thank you for "leading me not into temptation and delivering me from the evil one." Amen.

WITH GOD I CAN

"Not by might nor by power, but by my Spirit,"
says the LORD Almighty.

Zechariah 4:6

I can accomplish anything God wants me to do. My ability to do anything God asks me to do does not depend on how smart, strong, rich, or athletic I am.

My ability to please God is equal to the power of the Holy Spirit within me. I can do anything God asks of me as long as I learn to rely on his Spirit.

- - - - -

Philippians 4:13 says, "I can do all this through him who gives me strength." The work God has for me to do does not depend on my ability, only my "avail-ability." When I am determined to obey God, I can eliminate the words, "I can't" from my vocabulary.

QUESTIONS?

Why, my soul, are you downcast?
Why so disturbed within me? Put your hope in God,
for I will yet praise him, my Savior and my God.

Psalm 43:5

It's okay to question God when I don't understand something. At the same time, I can accept everything that happens to me, good or bad, because God can use it to make me a stronger person.

When I'm confused and don't understand, I need to be honest with God. "Why" is not a bad word. It's okay to ask questions, including asking for understanding. That's how I will learn.

———

Jesus, how do you want to use what's going on in my life right now? How can you use the good and the not-so-good stuff to make me more like you? Please show me today. Amen.

LOOKING UP

Let us look only to Jesus, the One who began
our faith and who makes it perfect.

Hebrews 12:2 NCV

People I trust will sometimes let me down. When
someone who claims to be a follower of Jesus
disappoints me, I need to be careful not to say, "Well, if
that's what a follower of Jesus is like, I don't want to be one!"

I always want to keep my eyes fixed on Jesus. He is the
only one who will never let me down.

Dear Jesus, help me to "fix my eyes on you" and to stay
focused on you as the example of how to think and act.
Create in me a loving heart, so I can forgive others
when they let me down. And help me remember that
sometimes I too let others down. Thank you for loving
and forgiving me. Amen.

I'LL GIVE IT MY ALL

"But be very careful to . . . love the LORD your God,
to walk in obedience to him, to keep his commands,
to hold fast to him and to serve him with
all your heart and with all your soul."

Joshua 22:5

What I do in life isn't the most important thing. I can be a teacher, explorer, scientist, a doctor, or anything I set my mind to become. What's most important is that whatever I choose to do, I do it out of a heart that wants to be my best for God. Then I can "do it with all my heart."

─ ─ ─ ─

God, sometimes I feel so very ordinary. I feel like my
"best" is pretty ho-hum. Maybe I'm not a world-class
athlete or a rock star waiting to be discovered. I'm just
me. But, God, could you help me be the best me I can
be? And help me do whatever I do with a heart that
wants to please you? Thanks, God. Amen.

GOTTA TELL SOMEBODY

"Now go; I will help you speak
and will teach you what to say."

Exodus 3:12

The better I know Jesus and the more I understand that his Holy Spirit lives in me, the more I will want to tell others about Jesus. I'll tell them he died for our sins, so we can be friends with God. Do I have a friend who needs to know about Jesus? Who might that be?

––––––

Jesus, I can tell my friends about you in simple ways,
like offering to pray for them and helping them in
meaningful ways. Telling my friends about you isn't
hard or complicated, but a lot of times I just don't think
about it. You're my best friend. Help me to think of
creative ways to introduce my other friends to my best
friend. Amen.

JESUS,
MY BEST FRIEND

You make known to me the path of life;
you will fill me with joy in your presence,
with eternal pleasures at your right hand.

Psalm 16:11

T he most wonderful thing about being a disciple
(a follower) of Jesus is his daily presence in my life.
No matter whether things are going great or not-so-great,
Jesus is with me. I can always enjoy his presence whether
things are going well or not so well. In fact, when things are
not going well, that's when I may feel he's closer than ever.

－－－－－

Jesus, today I'm going to try to imagine you right beside
me all day: at breakfast, at school, in the lunchroom,
on the playground, riding the bus, and at home. I know
you are always and everywhere present. I can never
NOT be in your presence. You're as close to me as the
air I breathe. Please help me be aware of your presence.
Amen.

HARD TIMES
ARE GOOD TIMES

"From this time forward I make you hear new things,
hidden things that you have not known."

Isaiah 48:6 NRSV

God will lead me through some difficult times. The difficult times help me learn new things about him. Real friendships grow deeper in difficult times. God wants to be my close friend; any difficulty that comes into my life can bring me closer to him.

God, sometimes I wish you were a "make-it-all-better" kind of God. I wish you could help me fast-forward through bad days and hit instant replay on good days. But sometimes you're more of a "wait-and-all-will-be-well" kind of God. I ask that you help me sort through my feelings, so I can make good choices and learn what you are trying to teach me. Amen.

LEARNING TO ASK

"Do you seek great things for yourself?
Do not seek them."

Jeremiah 45:5 NRSV

If I ask God to bless me and make me happy, I'm not asking God for what's most important. When I pray, I will ask God to help me know him better, to fill me with the Holy Spirit, and to give me the willingness to obey him always. True blessings and the deepest joy only come from knowing God. The closer I am to him, the happier I will be, no matter whether I always get what I want or not.

What I think will make me happy often isn't what actually makes me happy. Real happiness is to love and be loved. I can be happy just knowing that God loves me and I love him. Nothing can make me happier than knowing that!

I'LL ALWAYS TRUST GOD

Those who know your name trust in you, for you, LORD,
have never forsaken those who seek you.

Psalm 9:10

The secret of happiness is trust. The person who knows God, and knows God can be trusted, is the happiest person on the earth. Even if things don't always turn out the way I want them to, I can always make a choice to trust God. He never changes. He is always dependable!

– – – – –

Dear God, thank you for all you've given me. Thank you for the promise that you will be with me through every moment of every day. Thank you for loving me even when I'm not aware of your love. Amen.

SURPRISE!

"Do not worry about tomorrow,
for tomorrow will worry about itself.
Each day has enough trouble of its own."

Matthew 6:34

I will not worry about what's going to happen tomorrow or in the future. I'll remember God is in charge of my life, and he is full of good surprises. I'll let him surprise me with whatever he wants because I know he can use everything that happens, today or tomorrow, for my good.

I thank him for his surprises!

––––

God, I don't know what will happen today or tomorrow, but I do know all my todays and tomorrows are in your hands. Everything that happens, no matter what it looks like, will work out for the best. I trust you! Amen.

GOD GIVES ME LOVE

Dear friends, since God so loved us,
we also ought to love one another.

1 John 4:11

The Bible tells me that "God is love" and that love comes from God. But sometimes it's hard to love someone. Telling myself, "I'm going to treat that person with kindness and respect," doesn't help me love anyone.

When I pray, "Lord, give me your love for that person," then the Holy Spirit can help me.

He gives me the power to see that person as God sees them and to love them with God-like love.

Lord, it's hard for me to love _____. (Does anyone come to my mind?) I pray, "Holy Spirit, pour the love of God into my heart for _____." Asking God just once to give me his love for a person is a lot like taking only one vitamin—it doesn't hurt, but it doesn't do much good either. Asking the Holy Spirit to fill me with God's love is something I need to do every day, because every day I need God's help in loving others. Amen.

MAY

EARS TO HEAR GOD

Though you have not seen him, you love him;
and even though you do not see him now,
you believe in him and are filled with
an inexpressible and glorious joy.

1 Peter 1:8

Being a follower of Jesus is challenging because I'm following someone I cannot see. That's called "living by faith." Faith is all about believing that God is trustworthy, that Jesus is who he said he was, and that the Holy Spirit lives in me to help me know God's ways.

God wants to speak to me through his Word and through the voice of the Holy Spirit within me. Also, he can speak to me through the voice of his other followers. Am I listening?

———

Dear God, I know you are here, listening to me, caring about me, and loving me always. When I question or doubt your presence, help me remember that just because I can't see you doesn't mean you aren't real. Show me how to hear your voice. Teach me to listen. Amen.

IT'S WORTH WAITING

> By faith he [Moses] left Egypt,
> not fearing the king's anger; he persevered
> because he saw him who is invisible.
>
> *Hebrews 11:27*

Since I cannot see God, I'll need to learn to be patient. Patience is waiting for God to do the things I have asked of him. God might say: "Yes"; "No"; or "Wait." God wants me to trust him during these "waiting times," the times when I feel like he's not answering. Trusting while I wait for God to answer my prayer is called patience.

—————

Dear God, waiting for your answer to my prayer is as hard as waiting for summer vacation to begin. It always seems to take so long! I know I'm not very patient right now, but help me learn to be patient, especially when I want you to answer my prayers right away. Help me remember you're never late. You're always right on time, and I can wait. Amen.

WHAT DOES GOD THINK?

Am I now trying to win the approval of human beings, or
of God? Or am I trying to please people?
If I were still trying to please people,
I would not be a servant of Christ.

Galatians 1:10

Do I care more about what others think than what
God thinks? Sometimes God might clearly show me
something I need to do. Through reading his Word or by
the leading of the Holy Spirit, he will make his will known
to me. When that happens, I never need to ask myself,
"What will my friends or my family think?"

When I obey a word from God, what others think
doesn't matter. Only obedience matters. I will let God take
care of the people who misunderstand me.

- - - - -

O God, you know I care about the approval of others. I
want others to like me. Help me learn that what really
matters is staying true to you. If I do that, what others
think of me is in your hands. Amen.

TEACH ME TO TRUST

Even though I walk through the darkest valley,
I will fear no evil, for you are with me . . .

Psalm 23:4

When I pray for myself or someone else, God may answer my prayer in an unexpected way. He may take me or the other person through a difficult time. If that happens, I don't need to feel sorry for either one of us.

God uses difficult times to teach us about his faithfulness. He will see us through the good times and the bad.

God, help me learn that I won't always understand how you will answer my prayers. When I think I know how my prayers should be answered, help me remember that you are God, not me. You know better than I do. I'll put my trust in you every time! Amen.

POWER TO OBEY

When I am weak,
then I am strong.

2 Corinthians 12:10

Jesus will never ask me to do anything I cannot do with his help. When I feel weak and helpless, that is when Jesus wants to show me how powerful God is. The Holy Spirit within me will always give me the power to obey God. When I feel weak, I don't just want God to *give* me strength, I want him to *be* my strength. I want to learn how to tap into the power of the Holy Spirit within me.

- - - - -

God, help me learn to rely on your ability, not on how confident I feel about myself. I know feelings come and go. Sometimes I feel so confident, and other times I feel so weak. But, really, compared to your strength, all of my strength must seem weak and puny. Help me learn to live in complete dependence on your strength. Whether I feel confident or weak, help my strength come from you. Amen.

THE HOLY SPIRIT SPEAKS

> "Anyone who chooses to do the will of God
> will find out whether my teaching comes
> from God or whether I speak on my own."
>
> *John 7:17*

When I tell others about Jesus, I will be patient with them. I can't change their way of thinking. I can only ask the Holy Spirit to speak to their heart. A lot of the questions they have will only be answered *after* they decide to follow Jesus. I want to learn to be patient and let the Holy Spirit do his work.

The Holy Spirit can help them want to be a follower of Jesus so they will be "willing to do what God wants."

––––

Telling others about Jesus is like scattering seeds in the garden. I can't make the seeds grow. That's God's job. I can water the seed by showing others the love of God through the way I talk and act. After that, only God can make the seed grow in their heart.

A WISE WAY
TO PRAY

Clothe yourselves with humility
toward one another.

1 Peter 5:5

Here's a thought: sometimes my prayers about following Jesus might be self-centered. When I pray, "I am going to do great things for God!" the focus is on me.

Instead, I will pray, "O God, give me such a deep love for you that I will want to please you more than anyone or anything else on the earth."

If I love God like that, even the smallest acts of obedience will be great in his eyes.

———

Dear God, no matter what I'm doing—whether it seems important or not—I just want to please you. Whether I'm at school, playing at home, or hanging out with my friends, let the words of my mouth, the thoughts in my head, and everything I do and everywhere I go be acceptable to you. Amen.

HOLY LOVE

If you say, "The LORD is my refuge," and you make the
Most High your dwelling, no harm will overtake you,
no disaster will come near your tent.

Psalm 91:9–10

I can build my life on the truth that "God is love." He
is never not loving! Nothing can ever come into my
life that he cannot use to help me know him better. That
doesn't mean I will never have any troubles. It means God
will use those troubles to make me stronger in my faith.

If I allow him, he will use everything in my life to show
me how much he loves me.

— — — — —

God will never let anything stretch me to the breaking
point. When a rubber band is stretched, it holds things
together; without being stretched, the rubber band is
of little use. God created me to be stretched—to go
beyond my own strength—and trust his presence to
hold things together.

THINK ABOUT IT!

Because of the LORD's great love we are
not consumed, for his compassions never fail.
They are new every morning; great is your faithfulness.

Lamentations 3:22–23

The secret to staying excited about following Jesus is taking time to think about how great God is and how much he loves me. If I continue to do that, I will expect God to do greater things in and through me than he has ever done before.

- - - - -

Here's a prayer I can pray every morning: "O God, it's a beautiful day! You're so great! What incredible things are we going to do together today? Amen."

MAKE RIGHT TURNS

The fear of the LORD is the beginning of knowledge,
but fools despise wisdom and instruction.

Proverbs 1:7

Getting in the habit of doing the things I know are right is a good idea. Why? God does not do *for* me what he expects me to do *for myself*.

I must develop good habits. For example, working hard at whatever I do, obeying my parents, and always telling the truth are good habits to build. The more I practice doing what is right, the more natural it will become. God will help me if I just ask for his help.

God, give me the courage and patience to learn good habits in the same way I learned to ride my bike—by being willing to try again even when I try and fail. Fill my heart with a desire to do whatever it takes to please you in everything I do today. Amen.

OTHERS NEED LOVE

A new command I give you: Love one another.
As I have loved you, so you must love one another.

John 13:34

Do I love others the way God has loved me? Am I patient with their faults? Do I forgive them when they hurt me? The Holy Spirit shows me how much God loves me. He will also show me how important it is to learn to love others with that same love. And, the Holy Spirit is the one who gives me the ability to love like God loves. That's because he is the Spirit of God!

－ － － －

Dear Jesus, I really have a hard time loving _____ (tell God who that person is). Today, let me be willing to love this person. Lord, love this person through me. I ask that you would help me see him or her through your eyes. Give me a heart that forgives. I know this is possible since the Holy Spirit lives in me. He can pour your love into my heart. Lord, today I receive your love for this person. Amen.

MAKING HARD THINGS EASIER

We ought always to thank God for you . . .
because your faith is growing more and more, and the
love all of you have for one another is increasing.

2 Thessalonians 1:3

A good sign that the Holy Spirit is helping me grow up as a follower of Jesus is that it becomes easier to do the right things. For example, maybe I used to get upset with others easily; it may have been hard for me to be patient and forgiving. Now it is easier to forgive others. I thank God for any signs that the Holy Spirit is having his way in me and helping me be more loving.

God, I am growing and changing. Not in big, dramatic ways. But slowly, little by little, I can see you at work in me. Thank you, God, for doing with my willing heart what I couldn't do by myself. Amen.

A VERY SPECIAL VOICE

"I strive always to keep my conscience clear
before God and man."

Acts 24:16

C onscience is a big word for that small voice inside of
me that tells me what's right and wrong. When the Holy
Spirit lives inside me, he uses my conscience to tell me
what is and what is not pleasing to God.

My conscience can sometimes be the voice of God
within me. God's voice is so gentle that it is easy to ignore.
I want to get into the habit of obeying God's voice within
me. The more I obey this inner voice in the present, the
easier it will be to hear his voice in the future.

— — — — —

God, I'm afraid it's pretty easy for me to ignore your
voice. Are you in all those little thoughts that tell me
"this is right" or "this is wrong"? Is that your way of
getting my attention? If so, God, please teach me to pay
attention and obey. Amen.

TESTING, TESTING

I delight in weaknesses, in insults,
in hardships, in persecutions, in difficulties.
For when I am weak, then I am strong.

2 Corinthians 12:10

How well do I handle unpleasant experiences? My reaction is a test of how well I am doing as a follower of Jesus.

No matter how unpleasant an event may be, I will try to remember to pray, "Lord, I am happy to obey you in this experience. Thank you that it came my way. Help me to learn whatever it is you're trying to teach me." If God has allowed me to enter an unpleasant time, he is able to get me through it. The question is, will I trust him?

—————

Sometimes, God, when things aren't great, I whine and complain. I get angry, frustrated, and upset. Help me remember that you are in control—and with you, I can go through anything without complaining or getting angry. Amen.

DO IT GOD'S WAY

Where can I go from your Spirit? Where can
I flee from your presence? If I go up to the heavens,
you are there; if I make my bed in the depths,
you are there. If I rise on the wings of the dawn,
if I settle on the far side of the sea, even there your
hand will guide me, your right hand will hold me fast.

Psalm 139:7–10

E verything that happens to me, good or bad, can be
used by God to make me more like Jesus. Knowing
that, I can be ready to face anything that comes along.
It's not my job to tell God what needs to be done in my life.
My job is to submit to his will. Then he can do in me what
he wants. He has a purpose for everything that comes
along my way, good or bad. That purpose is to make me
more like Jesus.

— — — — —

God, I don't understand how you can be with me all the
time, but I know you are. And I don't understand how
you can use every event in my life—especially the bad
ones—for my good. But I know I can trust you. Help me
rest in your love and not feel like I need to understand
everything. Amen.

SEE THINGS FROM GOD'S VIEW

The God and Father of our Lord Jesus Christ,
the Father of compassion and the God of all comfort,
who comforts us in all our troubles, so that we
can comfort those in any trouble with the comfort
we ourselves receive from God.

2 Corinthians 1:3–4

F eeling sorry for myself doesn't do me or anybody else any good. When I feel sorry for myself, it is a sign that I am putting my personal comfort and happiness first, above everything else. Trusting God and feeling sorry for myself just don't go together.

God, I do feel sorry for myself sometimes. In school, when my friends go off and leave me at lunch, it hurts. When someone yells at me and I didn't do anything wrong, it hurts. I can't seem to make myself not feel sorry for myself. But I can come to you, tell you that I'm feeling pretty lousy, and then let it go. I know you can teach me something through both the good and the bad. Amen.

HEAVEN IS MY HOME

"My Father's house has many rooms . . .
I am going there to prepare a place for you."
John 14:2

J esus died and rose from the dead to make it possible for every human to have a friendship with God. When Jesus entered into heaven, he opened the door of heaven to anyone who follows him.

If I am a follower of Jesus, then he is preparing a place for me in heaven right now where I will be with him forever.

———

God, I don't know much about heaven. I kind of like it here right now. I'm wondering if following you is about bringing a little bit of heaven into my life every day. I think that's right! I bet I can bring a little bit of heaven with me wherever I go: in my home, at school, and every-where. That must be why you taught us to pray, "Your kingdom come, on earth as it is in heaven." Amen.

KNOWING GOD = LOVING GOD

> If you call out for insight and cry aloud
> for understanding, and if you look for it
> as for silver and search for it as for hidden treasure,
> then you will understand the fear of the LORD
> and find the knowledge of God.
>
> *Proverbs 2:3–5*

The great secret of life is that I don't become a better person by trying hard to act like a good person. I become a better person by allowing God to change me on the inside—in my heart.

The main thing is not improving my behavior but rather renewing my heart. I become my best for God by learning to serve him from my heart. The better I know God, the more I will want to please him. When my heart is full of love for God, my behavior is automatically better. The secret is knowing and loving him, not trying harder.

God, I want to do better. I want to be a more faithful follower of Jesus. Help me to know you better and to learn what doing my best to please you really means. Take my willing heart today. Amen.

WITH ME IN EVERYTHING!

"Do not fear, for I am with you; do not be dismayed,
for I am your God. I will strengthen you and help you."

Isaiah 41:10

God will not keep me out of trouble. He says, "I will be with you in trouble."

Sometimes when I am in trouble or having difficulty, I try so hard to get out of it. If I can learn to relax and quit trying so hard, I might hear God say to me, "I love you. I am with you. I won't let anything happen to you that you and I can't handle together."

———

God, today I am going to trust in your love. Whenever I feel unsure, confused, or full of questions, I'm going to whisper quietly to myself, "God, I am yours. I trust in you. I know you love me, and I have nothing to fear." Amen.

I'LL NEVER GIVE UP

"My sheep listen to my voice; I know them,
and they follow me. I give them eternal life,
and they shall never perish;
no one will snatch them out of my hand."

John 10:27–28

When it comes to growing as a follower of Jesus, I need to be patient with myself. When I trip up and fall down, I don't need to feel bad. I can just get up, thank God that he loves and forgives me, and go on enjoying my life with him.

God will never give up on me, so I'm not giving up on me either!

Dear God, is that really true . . . that you won't ever give up on me? Sometimes that is hard for me to believe, but if it weren't true, you wouldn't have sent Jesus to show me your love. God, help me accept the love you have for me. Then I can learn to love myself and others even when I feel unlovable. Amen.

FIRST THINGS FIRST

"Strive first for the kingdom of God
and his righteousness, and all these things
will be given to you as well."

Matthew 6:33

Jesus teaches me that the most important thing in life is my relationship with God. I am to put that first and everything else second. In fact, if I put him first in everything, all the things I am so concerned about will start to work out.

Am I doing that, or am I so concerned about so many other things that I don't take time for him?

— — — —

God, teach me what it means to put you first. I don't want anything else to be more important than what you and I have together. But there are so many things going on in my life that sometimes I forget about you. Help me to learn ways to keep my mind and heart focused on you no matter what I am doing. Amen.

THE BEST PLAN

"I pray also for those who will believe in me
through their message, that all of them may be one,
Father, just as you are in me and I am in you."

John 17:20–21

J esus prayed that I may be one with the Father as he is
one. Am I helping God answer that prayer, or do I have
other plans for my life?

The way to be one with God is to pray like Jesus
prayed, "Not my will but your will be done." I can ask God
to help me make sure my plans and his plans for my life are
the same—and that we are one.

Dear God, take my life, all of it. The good and the bad.
The happy and the sad. Let me live my life according
to your purpose—not mine—even when I really want
to do things my way. And God, your way is the best way!
Amen!

GOD CARES

Search me, God, and know my heart;
test me and know my anxious thoughts.

Psalm 139:23

I never need to worry. Worrying means I do not think God can take care of the details of my life.

If God cares for the millions of sparrows in the world, I'm pretty sure he will care for me. He knows exactly how many hairs are on my head! That's a pretty tiny detail. Why wouldn't I think he can take care of me?

— — — — —

God, I know I don't need to worry, but I do. So I'm going to practice just telling you everything I'm worried about. Then I'm going to leave my worries in your hands. Every time a worried thought comes into my mind, I'm giving it right back to you. You're bigger than any worry I might have. Thanks, God. Amen.

NO FEAR

"I am the LORD your God who takes hold
of your right hand and says to you,
Do not fear; I will help you."

Isaiah 41:13

A child of God never needs to fear. I don't need to be afraid of the dark, of being sick, or of what might happen in the future. I don't need to be afraid of someone bigger than me. I don't need to fear anything! I can trust God totally through anything that comes my way. He will help me.

— — — — —

God, I know I don't need to be afraid. I know you promise to care for me and watch over me. All I know to do, God, is to tell you when I'm afraid. Then I will ask you to fill my heart so full of your love that there's no room left over for fear. Amen.

HOW WILL I CHOOSE?

In the morning, LORD, you hear my voice;
in the morning I lay my requests before you
and wait expectantly.

Psalm 5:3

Following Jesus means learning to let God choose the steps I take. Sometimes I will make bad choices. Other times I may make choices that seem good to me, but they are not the choices God would have me make.

The only way to make the best choice is to live so close to my heavenly Father that I know in my heart, before I choose, what he would want me to do. If I stay close to him, I will know what will please him the most.

– – – – –

God, let my choices today be guided by your love. Let my thoughts be sheltered by your goodness. And let my hands and feet be the hands and feet of your loving kindness. What I really want to say, God, is today, let me be all yours. Amen.

I CAN PRAY ANYTIME

Pray at all times.

1 Thessalonians 5:17 GNB

I breathe all the time without thinking about it. Prayer is to my relationship with God what breathing is to my physical body. Without air I would die. Without prayer, my relationship with God suffers.

I want prayer to be as natural to me as breathing. I want to live in the presence of God and breathe his air.

— — — — —

Breathe on me, God. Help me learn to be so aware of your presence that I pray as naturally as I breathe. Fill me with your love with every breath I take today. Amen.

FILL ME UP!

This is how we know that we live in him
and he in us: He has given us of his Spirit.

1 John 4:13

The Holy Spirit came into me when I asked Jesus to be the Lord of my life. Because the Holy Spirit is God, I have the life of God in me.

I can allow the Holy Spirit to fill me so full that my every-day actions reflect the life of God in me. That's the way I become more like Jesus.

– – – – –

Holy Spirit, fill me so full of the life of God that, whether I'm playing, in school, or at home, his love will spill out all over those around me. Amen.

Q & A

"I have loved you with an everlasting love;
I have drawn you with unfailing kindness."

Jeremiah 31:3

Whenever I ask the question, "Why, God?" his answer is always the same, "Trust me. I love you so much." I never need to let my "whys" come between God and me.

It's okay for me to ask, "Why did such-and-such happen?" He loves answering, "Even though you don't understand right now, you can trust me. Can you be patient? I love you so much."

Am I hearing his answer?

———

God, if you love me so much, then why do some things hurt so much? Why do some days have to be so sad? Why do so many questions have to go unanswered? As I grow in my relationship with you, God, help me grow in understanding. Give me the faith to trust you even when I don't understand. Amen.

ANSWERED PRAYER

You will look for the LORD your God,
and if you search for him with all your heart,
you will find him.

Deuteronomy 4:29 GNB

The secret of getting my prayers answered is knowing the heart and mind of my heavenly Father.

The more I get to know him, the more clearly I understand how he thinks and feels about things. The more I know how he thinks and feels, the more natural it will become to pray according to his will.

———

God, separating what I want from what you want seems confusing to me right now. I think what I need to do is keep practicing the things that will help me know your voice better. Praying, listening, and reading your Word—those are the main things that will help me learn to trust you more. Amen.

OBEY GOD QUICKLY

"Come, follow me," Jesus said,
"and I will send you out to fish for people."
At once they left their nets and followed him.

Mark 1:17–18

I want to get into the habit of obeying Jesus whether it makes sense to me or not.

Jesus asked his first disciples to leave their jobs and follow him. That must have seemed risky to them at first, yet they obeyed.

Sometimes I won't understand how smart it is to obey God until after I have done it. I will never regret obeying God!

– – – – –

Jesus, what are you asking of me today? Give me open ears to hear and a willing heart to do whatever you ask me to do. Amen.

MY HEART, GOD'S HOME

Like newborn babies, crave pure spiritual milk,
so that by it you may grow up in your salvation,
now that you have tasted that the Lord is good.

1 Peter 2:2–3

God wants my heart to be a "Bethlehem," a place where Jesus is born.

Then, with Jesus at the center of my life, God wants to slowly grow me up until, more and more, I take on a likeness to the One who has been born in me.

Have I allowed Jesus to be born in me?

– – – – –

Jesus, be born in my heart like you were born in Bethlehem. I don't want my heart to be like the inn that Mary and Joseph were turned away from. The inn was too noisy and crowded to receive you. Let my heart be like the stable: warm and open. Let there always be room in my heart for you. Amen.

JUNE

GOD CHANGES HEARTS

"Whoever comes to me
I will never drive away."

John 6:37

There is no one—no matter how bad they are—who cannot be changed by God's power and love. There is no sin that God's love cannot forgive. There is not one person on the earth Jesus did not die for.

There is hope for everyone—including me!

Thank you, God, for your incredible love and power. Help me remember that not even the meanest kid or the worst criminal—no one—is beyond the reach of your love and power. You can rescue anyone from the bad things they have done and turn them into kind and loving people. When I see someone I don't like or someone I don't think is very nice, help me see them the way you see them. Amen.

GOD KEEPS ME SAFE

It is better to take refuge
in the L**ORD** than to trust in humans.

Psalm 118:8

A refuge is a shelter. It completely surrounds. God is a shelter for me. As a child of God, I can be sure that nothing will get through the shelter of God's love.

I am surrounded by the love of God. He will guard and keep me because of his great love for me.

– – – –

Dear God, keep me in the shelter of your love. Whether my life is sunny and warm or I feel like I'm caught in a threatening storm, be my unfailing shelter and refuge. Teach me, God, to trust in you. Amen.

WANTING
WHAT GOD WANTS

Now by this we may be sure that we know him,
if we obey his commandments.

1 John 2:3 NRSV

When I am a follower of Jesus, I want to know God's will. As I grow in my walk with him, I want to know God himself, as a closest friend.

When I really know God, the idea of choosing any other way but his isn't something I'll want to consider. In fact, my ordinary daily choices will normally be God's will for me, because I make them in fellowship with him.

———

God, draw me close to you. Let the friendships I have and the choices I make draw me closer to you. Even when I'm busy or tired or feeling overwhelmed, teach me how to let everything I experience draw me closer to you. Amen.

I CAN HEAR GOD

I will never leave you or forsake you.
Hebrews 13:5 NRSV

D o I really believe what God says in his Word, or do I believe in my fears? God's Word says, "'I will never leave you or forsake you.' So we can say with confidence, 'The Lord is my helper; I will not be afraid. What can anyone do to me?'" (Hebrews 13:5–6 NRSV).

Have I really heard God say that to me? Not just in my Bible but to me? Do I really believe it or am I still full of fear?

— — — — —

Lord, help me to hear your words to me, not just read it in my Bible. When I'm afraid or anxious or just not happy, help me hear your voice of love. Help me to hear you more loudly than the "voices" inside me that are making me feel bad. Amen.

FREE FROM FEAR

The LORD is with me, I will not be afraid;
what can anyone do to me?

Psalm 118:6 GNB

God says, "I will never leave you." I can say, "I will not fear." This doesn't mean I won't feel afraid at times, but I can take a deep breath, remember what God has said, and then declare, "I will not fear!"

Is there something I'm afraid of right now? What is it? I can look straight at my worst fear right now and say, "The Lord is my helper, I will not fear!"

───────

You, Lord, are my helper. Because I trust in your love, I will not fear. Give me the courage I need to face my fears and then say with a confident voice, "The Lord is my helper, I will not be afraid!" Amen.

WALKING WITH GOD

How I love to do your will, my God!
I keep your teaching in my heart.
Psalm 40:8 GNB

The fact that I am a child of God means I have God's life inside me. God in me is working with me to help me want what he wants.

As I grow in my relationship with God, his will and my will can become almost the same. Obeying him can become as natural as breathing.

———

God, I want more of you and less of me. Be at work in my life that each day I can be shaped and molded into who you want me to be. Amen.

JESUS IS LORD

"I am the vine, you are the branches.
Those who abide in me and I in them bear much fruit,
because apart from me you can do nothing."

John 15:5 NRSV

A m I serious about following Jesus?
Am I becoming more and more connected to him?

Is Jesus the center of my life, or are other activities squeezing him out?

Do I live like I want to depend on him, or am I okay living my life without his help?

⎯ ⎯ ⎯ ⎯

O Jesus, be the center of my life. Be more important than anything else. Teach me what it means to "abide" in you. Then show me how to do that every day. Amen.

NO HOLDING BACK

This is love: that we walk in obedience to
his commands. As you have heard from the beginning,
his command is that you walk in love.

2 John 1:6

The way to know more of God's will for me is to do what I already know is right.

Am I holding back on doing something God wants me to do? Or am I doing anything I know makes him sad? Is there anything I need to make right? Have I hurt anyone? Do I need to ask someone to forgive me?

Until I do the things I know God wants, I will not take the next step of growth. I'll make this my motto: Obey God Now!

God, help me do the simple things today I know will please you: obey my parents, be kind to others, and seek to know you more. As I do what I already know pleases you, show me how I can please you even more. Amen.

GOD'S LIFE MAKES ME RICH

"Blessed are the poor in spirit,
for theirs is the kingdom of heaven."

Matthew 5:3

To be poor in spirit means I understand I have nothing God did not give me. And I know whatever I need will come from him.

When I pray knowing how poor and needy I am apart from him, God will answer. To be poor in spirit means to be rich (the most blessed) in what really matters.

Because I am God's child, I can share in the riches of his love. Everything he has is mine because I am his!

— — — — —

God, the more I get to know you, the more I think when it comes to living in your "kingdom," everything is backward from what seems to make sense. The Bible says things like "the poor are rich," "the weak are strong," and "the least are the greatest." I think I'm going to need a lot more time before I understand this stuff. Holy Spirit, keep teaching me. I want to learn! Amen.

THE RIGHT REASONS

You ask and do not receive,
because you ask wrongly, in order to spend
what you get on your pleasures.

James 4:3

I t is possible to pray for the wrong reason. The wrong
reason to pray for something is, "just because I want it."
The right reason to ask God for something is "because you
want me to have it."

I want to learn how to want what God wants instead of
always thinking of myself first. I always want to say, "Your
will be done," and not "My will be done."

— — — — —

God, sometimes I want something so badly I don't even
think about what you want for me. I just want what I
want. Show me how to line my will up with yours, so I
can learn how to make my wants the same as your wants
for me. Amen.

LETTING GO

Take delight in the LORD,
and he will give you the desires of your heart.

Psalm 37:4

Surrendering my life over to God means I can happily let go of my own "wants." I can honestly pray, "Your will be done."

When I do this, I discover that what God wants for me is much better than what I often want for myself. In fact, when I surrender fully to God, I find that he not only gives me many of the things I want, but he also gives me new desires.

He helps me want the things he wants for me.

- - - - -

God, I know sometimes you can't be delighted in the things you see me doing or saying. I can be selfish, stubborn, impatient, and crabby. Forgive me, God, when I make my wants and needs more important than what you want for me. Today, God, let the desires of my heart be pleasing to you. Show me how to "delight" in your will. Amen.

GIVE THANKS

Just as you received Christ Jesus as Lord,
continue to live your lives in him, rooted and built up
in him, strengthened in the faith as you were taught,
and overflowing with thankfulness.

Colossians 2:6–7

Pride is putting what I want ahead of what God wants for me. It means I think I'm more important than God and that my way is better than his.

To be "rooted and built up in him" means to accept God's will for my life thankfully, continually, and every day—even when something happens I don't understand.

———

Thank you, Lord, for working out your will in my life. Help me to "overflow with thankfulness," even in the middle of something that makes me sad or mad. I know a big part of being "built up" in you—in other words, growing—is learning to be thankful in everything. I can do that because I know you know what's best. Amen.

LIVING WATER

"Whoever believes in me, as Scripture has said,
rivers of living water will flow from within them."
By this he meant the Spirit, whom those who
believed in him were later to receive.

John 7:38–39

When I committed my life to Jesus, the Holy Spirit came into me. Jesus said the Holy Spirit is like a river of fresh water that flows out from deep inside of me.

People are thirsty for God. Living my life for God is like being a source of pure cold water to all the thirsty people around me. People long to satisfy the inner thirst they have for God. I can show them how to do that by learning to allow the river of the Holy Spirit to flow out of me in all I do.

— — — — —

Lord, I want to be so full of the Holy Spirit that he overflows onto those around me: my family, my teachers, and my friends—everyone. Let my life be like pure water that gives thirsty souls a fresh drink of God. Amen.

CLOSE TO JESUS

"If you keep my commands, you will remain in my love,
just as I have kept my Father's commands and remain
in his love. I have told you this so that my joy may be
in you and that your joy may be complete."

John 15:10–11

I t doesn't matter what circumstance I find myself in. I
can be just as close to Jesus in any ordinary daily event
as I can in church.

Staying close to Jesus and having a sense of his
presence isn't dependent on my outward experiences. It is
something that happens inside of me, in my heart and my
mind. I want to stay close to Jesus wherever I am. I want to
learn what it means to "remain in his love" at all times.

⸺ ⸺ ⸺ ⸺

Jesus, today I'm going to try to imagine you are right
beside me everywhere I go. If I'm riding in the car, you
are sitting next to me. If I'm playing outside, you are
playing right beside me. Wherever I am and whatever
I'm doing, help me picture you right there with me.
Jesus, make a difference in the way I act and think
today. Amen.

NEW LIFE, NEW HABITS

"After that, he poured water into a basin
and began to wash his disciples' feet, drying them
with the towel that was wrapped around him."

John 13:5

When I am born again I receive the life of God in me. I will want to form new habits that line up with the new life God has placed in me. I will want to do God's will.

I don't need to look for something big to do for God. I just need to do the little, ordinary, daily things with a desire to please him.

––––

Jesus, today I'm going to act as if washing the disciples' feet means being ready to do whatever is needed, wherever I am. I'll just practice being a servant all day. If my mom wants me to set the table, help me be willing. If my brother or sister need help with something, I'll be right there. Help me be a foot-washing kind of kid today! Amen.

LIVING FOR JESUS

"Greater love has no one than this:
to lay down one's life for one's friends."

John 15:13

Being a friend of Jesus means I will lay down my life for him. That doesn't mean I will have to die for him as he did for me.

"Laying down *my* life" means "picking up *his* life." It means that I will be willing to "die" to my desire to simply please myself and be "alive" to the things that please God.

— — — — —

Jesus, I give as much of me as I honestly can to as much of you as I understand. "Laying down my life" isn't something I can do all at once. I do it each day as I grow deeper in my understanding of you. Thank you for being so patient with me as I learn what it means to follow you.

I'LL BE CAREFUL
WHAT I SAY

"Do not judge,
or you too will be judged."

Matthew 7:1

Jesus only had one thing to say about judging or criticizing others: "Don't do it!" Judging others means I think I am better than they are. I am not.

Once I see how far I fall short of God's standard, I won't feel like I can judge anyone. I will ask God—the only Judge—to have mercy on me.

— — — —

Lord Jesus Christ, have mercy on me. Forgive me when I'm critical of others. Forgive me when I think I'm better than others. Forgive me when I forget to be compassionate and fall into the temptation of making fun of others. Today, give me your love for every person I meet. Amen.

GOD WILL
GET ME THROUGH

When he [Peter] saw the wind, he was afraid
and, beginning to sink, cried out, "Lord, save me!"
Immediately Jesus reached out his hand and caught
him. "You of little faith," he said, "why did you doubt?"

Matthew 14:30–31

I never need to worry about how rough things get around
me. I never need to be afraid of what is going to happen.
Jesus is always able to reach out his hand and get me
through whatever comes along.

The same God who helped Peter walk on the water will
also help me walk on top of whatever happens to me, right
now and always.

— — — — —

God, if you kept Peter from sinking when he was doing
something that seems impossible—walking on water—
I guess you can keep me from going under too. When I
find it hard to believe you are really in control, keep my
faith afloat. Amen.

A REAL FRIEND

"You are my friends if you do what I command."
John 15:14

Being a real friend of Jesus doesn't mean just believing certain ideas about him. "Faith without works" is a dead faith. Real friends do things together; they don't just talk. They care deeply about what each other thinks and feels.

Believing the right things is very important. But if Jesus and I have a real friendship, it will be more than simply having the right ideas. I will naturally want to do things that please him.

––– ––– –––

Jesus, I know we're best friends. And I know that, because we're best friends, we always want the best for each other. There's no question in my mind that you always want the best for me and that you love me so much. Help me be just as good a friend to you as you are to me. Amen.

OTHERS
NEED MY PRAYER

We ask our God to make you
worthy of the life he has called you to live.
May he fulfill by his power all your desire for
goodness and complete your work of faith.

2 Thessalonians 1:11 GNB

An important part of my relationship with God is praying for others—asking God to help them live worthy of the life he created them to live.

God wants me to pray for others so I don't get too centered on my own needs. Jesus always thought of others first. Seeing God answer my prayers for others will bring me more joy than getting my own needs met.

Who should I pray for right now? Jesus, right now I pray for _____. Please take care of them, watch over them, let them know how much you love them, and give them your peace. Amen.

OTHERS
NEED MY CARE

"As for me, far be it from me that I should sin
against the LORD by failing to pray for you."

1 Samuel 12:23

Asking God to give me a desire to pray for others is a
step toward learning to love others as God loves me.
I can pray for my family, friends, and other people I know
who have needs.

The more I pray for others, the less I will be worried
about getting my own needs met. A sign that I am growing
more like Jesus is that I am thinking about others first.

Jesus, it's easy to pray for my mom and my dad, because
I know sometimes they get really tired and they do a
lot for me. It's easy to pray for my friends because I'm
always thinking about them. But, Jesus, it's hard to
know who else to pray for or even what to say when I
do pray for someone. God, show me who you want me to
pray for, and, while you're at it, could you help me know
how to pray when I do pray for them? Amen.

OTHERS NEED
MY FORGIVENESS

"My command is this:
Love each other as I have loved you."
John 15:12

Jesus said, "Don't judge others." I don't want to criticize others and wish they would get what they deserve. I want to be loving and forgiving toward them like God has been toward me.

I'm glad God forgives me and doesn't punish me when I do wrong. With God's help I want to treat others the way he has treated me: with love and forgiveness and never with judgment and criticism.

God, sometimes being loving is hard. Thinking of myself first comes a lot more easily than putting others first. Help me treat others the way you have treated me. Help me be forgiving when I feel angry. Help me be thoughtful and kind when I want to rush to the head of the line and things like that. Help me be the person you created me to be. Amen.

GOD IN, SIN OUT

You are to think of yourselves as dead,
so far as sin is concerned, but living
in fellowship with God through Christ Jesus.

Romans 6:11 GNB

The reason Jesus died on the cross was not only to forgive my sins but to give me power over sin too. Either God will rule in my life, or sin will rule.

If I continually give in to sinful choices, then sin will rule. If I allow God's love and life to rule in me, the sinful desires will die. I must make a choice.

— — — —

O God, I know I must make a choice. Please show me how to let your life live in me so that sin will lose its power over me. I want you to rule in my life, not sin. So, help me surrender to you today, tomorrow, and every day. Amen.

SIN IS DANGEROUS

"Lead us not into temptation,
but deliver us from the evil one."

Matthew 6:13

The presence of evil in the world is real. If I do not learn to recognize the power of darkness, I will have a harder time living in the light of God's truth.

I always want to be on guard against doing or saying something bad. The power of the Holy Spirit in me will help me walk in the light of God's love. The Spirit will help me overcome the darkness of the evil one.

God, let the light of your love shine bright in my life. No matter what evil is present in the world around me, I know your love is greater. Help me overcome the darkness in the world around me by shining your light wherever I go. Amen.

THANKFUL FOR TRIALS

The Lord disciplines the one he loves.

Hebrews 12:6

There will always be sin in the world. There will always be suffering. But because I'm a follower of Jesus, the suffering is not necessarily a meaningless accident. It can be a means God uses to teach me—or the one suffering—more about his loving care for me.

If I want to go deep in my understanding of God, I can expect to go through difficult times. God never makes bad things happen to me, but he can always use bad things as a part of his loving plan to grow my trust in him. He may even use those things to discipline me—to give me a "time out" to help me focus my attention on him instead of what's happening around me.

––––––

Jesus, the idea of suffering is scary. I don't even like to think about suffering. I'd rather read Bible verses about joy and gladness and singing. But I do want to live my life for you. If I get scared about the future, God, help me remember you're with me today, and you will be with me in all my tomorrows, no matter what they bring me. Amen.

GOD IS ENOUGH

My child, do not despise the LORD's discipline or
be weary of his reproof, for the LORD reproves the one
he loves, as a father the son in whom he delights.

Proverbs 3:11–12 NRSV

During the most difficult times, I will learn the most
about God's goodness.

No matter how difficult my circumstances, I can learn
to draw on the grace and love of God to get me through.
He is always with me.

I can never NOT be in God's presence. His presence is
enough for everything I will ever go through.

When was the last time I went through something
difficult or was afraid, lonely, or sad? What happened?
Did I pray about it? Did I learn something about God by
going through it?

— — — — —

Dear God, next time I'm facing something difficult,
remind me that you're right there and I can talk it over
with you. I know you never send anything bad my way.
And I know even though you didn't send it, you can use
it. Help me face difficult events knowing you can use
any event to teach me more about you and grow my
faith. Amen.

GOD DOESN'T MAKE MISTAKES

Guard my life, for I am faithful to you;
save your servant who trusts in you.
You are my God.

Psalm 86:2

When I let God guard my life, I never have to try to control everything. If I do, I will be frustrated. But if I trust God to guard my life, I can relax.

I know he'll take care of anything and everything that comes my way. God can always make everything turn out for my good, no matter how things seem to be going at the moment.

- - - - -

God, today I trust in you. Tomorrow I may forget I said that, but for today, I trust in you. Remind me tomorrow if I do forget, because I think this is seriously important to keep in mind. It helps me relax, and it must please you to see that I'm okay with you being in charge. Amen.

GOD HAS A PLAN

I press on to take hold of that
for which Christ Jesus took hold of me.

Philippians 3:12

God's plan is to give me a special work in his kingdom. It will be a job he has specially prepared and gifted me for. And he can give me everything I need to accomplish it.

When I ask God to show me his plan for my life, I can commit myself to going after it with everything I've got. After all, this is the only way I will be truly satisfied.

I always want to remember this, "God is preparing *me* for what he is preparing *for* me."

– – – – –

What do I want to be when I grow up? Sometimes I daydream about that. Some people think daydreaming is wasting time, but in the Bible God frequently spoke through dreams. My daydreams are a gift from God. He's planting seeds of what he might call on me to do when I'm bigger. Since he loves me so much, he must have something really special for me. I can hardly wait to see what God has for me to do!

MAKING GOD SMILE

No one serving as a soldier gets entangled
in civilian affairs, but rather tries
to please his commanding officer.

2 Timothy 2:4

When the Holy Spirit lives in me, there will be things I refuse to do. These things might not be sinful but doing them keeps me from sensing God's pleasure.

"Pleasing God" will be the test for everything I do. Before doing anything, I will always ask, "Will it please God if I do this?" If the answer is "No," I won't do it!

— — — —

God, I honestly don't know sometimes what you want me to do and what you don't want me to do. Lying, stealing, cheating, or being rude . . . well, those are obviously not what you would want. But other things aren't always so easy to see. Give me eyes that see right from wrong and a heart that feels your pleasure or pain. I really want to know what will make you smile. Amen.

A GOOD NIGHT'S SLEEP

Create in me a pure heart, O God,
and renew a steadfast spirit within me.
Restore to me the joy of your salvation.

Psalm 51:10, 12

When I sin, I'll confess it quickly. I won't wait! I want to always keep my heart pure.

The presence of unconfessed sin in my life can keep me from the joy of having a sense of God's presence with me. I especially don't want go to sleep at night without talking to God about anything that has come between us during the day.

God, I think tonight when I go to bed, I'll just tell you my "highs and lows" from the day. I'll pray about the things I felt good about and the things that weren't so good. Then I'll ask you to forgive me for anything I said or did that makes me uncomfortable to think about. I never want anything to come between you and me that makes you feel sad. Amen.

JULY

NO EXCUSES

*Confess your sins to each other
and pray for each other so that you may be healed.*

James 5:16

I won't try to get myself "off the hook" with God by trying to explain away my sins. The only way to get free from the bad feeling sin creates in my heart is to simply be honest with God about it.

I won't argue with God, ignore him, or try to defend myself. I'll just confess my sin.

Sometimes it might be helpful to confess my sin to another person I trust and have them pray for me. God will forgive and cleanse me. The feeling of his presence and peace will return to my heart.

God, I don't ever want to let my heart feel distant from you. Show me anything that separates me from your love and anything I need to confess. I ask for your forgiveness, God. Amen.

DEEP LOVE FOR JESUS

"Love the Lord your God
with all your heart and with all your soul
and with all your mind and with all your strength."

Mark 12:30

I want my love for Jesus to be strong and personal. I don't just want to admire him from a distance and try to follow his teachings. If I have a passionate love for Jesus, that will enable me to follow him from my heart.

Only the Holy Spirit can pour that kind of love into my heart.

— — — — —

Lord Jesus, help me love you with all my heart, soul, and mind. Create in me a deep, passionate love for you, a love that will grow deeper and stronger. Amen.

GOD'S SPOTLIGHT

You show me the path of life.
In your presence there is fullness of joy;
in your right hand are pleasures forevermore.

Psalm 16:11 NRSV

It is easy to say, "Oh, yes, I know I am a sinner," because everybody is a sinner. But when I come into God's presence, he doesn't let me get by that easy.

He says, "What about this particular sin?" God gets specific and asks me to confess in detail.

If I confess what God shows me, I will come into a sense of his presence unlike anything I've ever experienced before. I want to learn to live continually in his presence.

God, I know when I'm crabby or when I'm angry. I know when I want things to go my way. But other times I really don't know when I've done something I need to confess. God, when I'm blind to my own sinfulness, open my eyes. Create in me a clean heart, O God. Amen.

WHAT REALLY MATTERS

There is no fear in love. But perfect love drives out fear,
because fear has to do with punishment.
The one who fears is not made perfect in love.

1 John 4:18

I never have to worry if I am a child of God. Worry is caused by my fear that things aren't going to work out the way I want them to.

If I really want God's will and not my own, I can be at peace regardless of what comes my way. My ability to trust him and relax does not depend on what happens or doesn't happen.

Being free of fear and worry depends on keeping my focus on him and trusting him completely. I want my love for God to grow so much that it chases away all fear.

— — — —

God, I do trust in you, but sometimes I still worry. How can I be afraid or worry when I know you're by my side? Teach me how to let your love fill my heart so completely that there's no room for worry or fear. Amen.

WHAT TO
DO WITH WORRY

"Who of you by worrying can add
a single hour to your life?"

Luke 12:25

God will not keep me from worrying.
Jesus said, "Let not your heart be troubled." Not worrying is something I can do only by the power of Jesus living in me. I can tell myself a hundred and one times a day, "I will not let myself worry" and it won't keep me from worrying.

Until I learn to trust God in the middle of whatever is happening to me, I'll just keep on worrying. Jesus says, "Don't worry." So it must be possible to not worry. He wouldn't tell me not to do something if it wasn't possible to stop doing it!

- - - -

God, fill my heart and soul with the ability to let go of worry and grab hold of your love. Today, God, anytime worrisome thoughts begin to crowd in, I'm going to say over and over, "Let your love overcome my fear . . . Let your love overcome my fear . . . Let your love overcome my fear." Amen.

MY LIFE
IS IN GOD'S HANDS

You, LORD, are our Father. We are the clay,
you are the potter; we are all the work of your hand.

Isaiah 64:8

I want my life to be like a lump of soft clay in the potter's hands. God is the potter, and he has a vision of the beautiful sculpture into which I can be shaped. God may want to use difficult circumstances and relationships to press me and squeeze me into the kind of image he has in mind.

Will I let him do that?

— — — —

Dear God, I will never be satisfied with anything less than being shaped by your loving hands. Mold my heart, shape my soul, and fill my mind with wisdom that I may be used by you today and every day. Amen.

SAYING "NO," SAYING "YES"

"The gate is narrow and the road is hard
that leads to life, and there are few who find it."

Matthew 7:14 NRSV

Jesus never said it would be easy to be his follower.
If I really want to be my best for God, it will cost me
something. I will not be able to do everything I want to do.
Saying yes to God means I will have to learn to say no to
some things. The only way to be my best for God is to always
say, "Yes!" (to him).

O God, I want to find the road that leads to the best
life you have to offer. I know it won't always be easy.
It might not even be what I always want for myself.
But I know you love me and you're with me. I want to
trust you so completely that each day begins as a new
adventure. Wherever you lead me and whatever doors
you open, I'm going with you. Amen.

FOLLOWING
GOD'S FOOTSTEPS

"Choose for yourselves this day
whom you will serve."

Joshua 24:15

I t is not necessary for me to know exactly where God is leading me.

It is only important for me to say, "I will follow you no matter where you lead me." It doesn't matter where he leads me. It only matters that I am with him.

Choosing to follow God means choosing to be faithful, even when I don't know how things will turn out.

— — — —

Jesus, today I choose to follow you. I may forget that
I made that choice! If I forget, get my attention and
remind me that even the littlest choices matter to you.
Amen.

I'M NEVER
TOO YOUNG

"As for me and my household,
we will serve the Lord."

Joshua 24:15

Will I serve the Lord? Will I make that choice?
Serving God means waiting on him and learning to
know what he wants me to do, then doing it with a joyful
heart. No matter how young or weak I am, I can choose to
serve the Lord.

I can imagine that I'm a waiter in a restaurant. I see
Jesus come in the door and take a seat at a table. When I
go over to his table, I'll say, "How may I serve you?"

In other words, I'm asking, "God, what would you like?"
That's what it means to serve God. What does he want of
me? What can I bring him? How can I serve him so that he
is satisfied?

— — — — —

Lord, help me learn to wait on you like a good servant.
Amen.

GIVE IT AWAY

Let us not give up the habit of meeting together,
as some are doing. Instead, let us encourage
one another all the more.

Hebrews 10:25 GNB

The church is not simply a building I visit. The church is a gathering of followers of Jesus anywhere and anytime. We gather for the purpose of encouraging one another and serving the world.

The reason a campfire burns so brightly is because all the logs are together. If I take a log out of the fire and set it aside by itself, it will die out quickly.

I cannot be a disciple of Jesus by myself. I need other followers of Jesus in my life in order to grow.

—————

Lord, if I am going to "burn brightly" for you, I know I will need to spend some time regularly with other followers of Jesus. I will need to be encouraged, and I will want to encourage others. Together is what it's all about! Amen.

I HAVE A GIFT

Use whatever gift you have received
to serve others.

1 Peter 4:10

I do not need to be too concerned about who I am or what gifts and talents I have.

If I will concentrate on knowing Jesus, he will use every gift he has given me to bless others. One main purpose of the gifts God has given me is to strengthen and encourage other followers of Jesus.

Then we can all reach out together to those who don't know him and need to be touched by his love.

— — — — —

Jesus, you made me just the way I am. So, there must be something special about me. Help me, Jesus, grow in understanding what my gifts are. Show me how I can use those gifts to reach others who need to know you. Amen.

GIFTS
ARE FOR OTHERS

Do not let any unwholesome talk come
out of your mouths, but only what is helpful
for building others up according to their needs,
that it may benefit those who listen.

Ephesians 4:29

As I continue to faithfully follow Jesus, I will become more like him personally. The more like him I become, the bigger blessing I can be to those around me.

The best way to bless others is to be wholly dedicated to God and use the gifts and abilities he has given me to serve them.

— — — —

God, when I'm with other friends who are trying to follow you, help me be an encourager. Help me always try to say things that build people up and not the kind of words that tear them down. Whether I use words or whether I just serve without saying anything, teach me how to use whatever gifts you have given me to bless others. Amen.

ALL FOR GOD, ALL THE TIME

"Suppose one of you wants to build a tower.
Won't you first sit down and estimate the cost
to see if you have enough money to complete it?"

Luke 14:28

There is a price to pay to be my best for God.
My priority must be: God first, God second, and God third. Nothing else and no one else matters as much as knowing and following him. Am I willing—really willing—to put God first?

The best way I can show others that I care about them is to care most about God. Putting God first means everybody else matters, because they matter to him.

———

Jesus, sometimes I'm afraid no matter how hard I try, I won't be able to be my best for you. Sometimes I think what you ask of me is too much. I pray I'll be willing to give you my whole life—past, present, and future. I can't even imagine how much you must love me. I want to do whatever it takes and pay whatever price to be my best for you. Amen.

TREAT PEOPLE
LIKE JESUS DID

"Do not resist an evil person.
If anyone slaps you on the right cheek,
turn to them the other cheek also."

Matthew 5:39

Jesus never demanded to be treated fairly. He didn't insist on being treated like he was the Son of God.

If I want to be like Jesus, I will need to be willing to be misunderstood, just like he was. When I am misunderstood, treated unfairly, or insulted, God can help me see those times as opportunities to grow to be more like Jesus. The Spirit of Jesus in me can help me be kind and loving, even to those who mistreat me.

———

Jesus, if someone is mean to me today, help me walk away without wanting to get even or say something back. If someone is unkind, help me be loving and kind in return. And if someone picks on me, help me respond the way you would. Amen.

CARING IS GIVING

I have become all things to all people
so that by all possible means I might save some.

1 Corinthians 9:22

Here are two important questions I want to think and pray about today: Am I praying for those who are not following Jesus? Am I doing or saying anything that could help others want to know Jesus?

Only the Holy Spirit can give me a desire to help others discover the love of God that I have found. I want to let God use me in any way he can to introduce them to my best friend.

-- -- -- -- --

Dear Lord, give me a special love for those who don't know you. And place the desire in my heart to see them come to know you. Show me how to share your love with them. Amen.

GOD KNOWS
ALL ABOUT IT

"Consider the ravens: They do not sow or reap,
they have no storeroom or barn; yet God feeds them.
And how much more valuable you are than birds!"

Luke 12:24

I want to continually remember that God is aware of everything that happens to me. When difficulty comes I can just say, "It's all right. My Father knows all about it."

God loves me, and I can never think of anything he has not already thought of. I'm more important to him than birds, and he cares about them! So, why should I worry?

— — — —

Today, I'll take a minute to picture holding in my hands whatever is troubling me. Then I'll raise my hands to the sky and offer it up to God. I'll watch as a bigger pair of hands—God's—surround mine. I'll imagine letting go of what's in my hands and leaving it in God's. That is the best place to leave anything that's worrying me—in the big hands of my loving Father in heaven.

WHAT DO OTHERS SEE IN ME?

I am not ashamed of the gospel,
because it is the power of God that
brings salvation to everyone who believes.

Romans 1:16

Others will not be drawn to God because they see how smart, talented, or clever I am. People will come to Jesus by seeing God's love in me and by the power of the Holy Spirit in me.

Sharing God's Word boldly with people and praying that the Holy Spirit will draw them to Jesus is something I can do no matter how young I am.

When Jesus was on the earth, he didn't tell people to go to church. He asked them to hang out with him and to follow him. Then they could experience what he was really like and have a relationship. Jesus didn't criticize; he loved and cared and listened. That's the best way to let others know what Jesus is like: to follow his example by loving, caring, and paying attention to what's happening in others' lives. How can I put Jesus' love into action today?

REAL POWER

If anyone is in Christ, the new creation has come:
The old has gone, the new is here!
2 Corinthians 5:17

The truth about Jesus Christ is so powerful it can change a person instantly. They can change from being a self-centered sinner into a God-centered child of heaven.

The moment someone prays sincerely, "Jesus, you are the Son of God and my Lord. I will obey you," the Holy Spirit enters his or her life. He can begin to change their heart and give them a desire to please God.

I want the Holy Spirit to help me learn how to introduce people to Jesus. God, thank you that when I said yes to you, the Holy Spirit came inside me. Because you live inside me, I have the power—your power—to do your will. You are changing me from the inside out. I want to be and do what you want me to be and do. I want to be my best for you. Amen.

THE WAY TO LIVE

This is love for God: to obey his commands.
And his commands are not burdensome,
for everyone born of God overcomes the world.

1 John 5:2–4

Jesus doesn't force me to obey him.
He reveals the truth to me—that he is the Son of God.
When I really understand who Jesus is, I cannot help but
obey him. I will gladly call him "Lord." It's not hard to obey
someone you love—someone who loves you that much!

Jesus, you gave your life, so I could have mine. That kind
of love is more than I can understand. Thank you for
the gift of life, for the gift of this day, and for the gift of
your love. Let me live this day thanking you, even if it's
a lousy, terrible, no-good, and very bad day. Remind me
that you still love me and are with me. Amen.

"WAIT"
DOESN'T MEAN "LATE"

I wait for the Lord more than
watchmen wait for the morning.

Psalm 130:6

It is important for me to "wait on the Lord." That's when I learn how to come into God's presence.

Prayer is not mainly about asking God for things, but about getting to know God. Then I understand how he feels about the things I'm asking for.

When I know God's heart, I will ask according to God's will. And I can only know God's heart by waiting on him and spending time with him.

————

God, teach me what it means to "wait" on you. Show me your heart—how you feel about things—and let me grow in knowing you. Amen.

MORE THAN A TEACHER

His divine power has given us everything
we need for a godly life through our knowledge
of him who called us by his own glory and goodness.

2 Peter 1:3

I f I know Jesus only as a great teacher, his teachings will discourage me. They are too hard.

But when I am born again, I see that Jesus did not come just to teach. Jesus came to make me into what he teaches I should be. And that is the work of the Holy Spirit in me.

The Holy Spirit works in me to help me want to do what he wants me to do. Then I can work out what he has worked in me.

— — — —

God, sometimes the teachings of Jesus sound like "Mission Impossible"! If, by my own strength, I could do all the things Jesus says to do, I wouldn't need Jesus in the first place. But, God, you change me from the inside out. That's how I learn to want what you want for me. Thank you, Lord!

GOD MORE,
THINGS LESS

Since we have died with Christ,
we believe that we will also live with him.

Romans 6:8 NRSV

God wants me to be so totally focused on him that I can be described as "dead" to everything that doesn't really matter. In other words, outside of God's will, nothing else influences me. That seems so hard to imagine. But as I begin to know him more deeply, other things do seem much less important.

– – – – –

God, being "dead" to anything doesn't sound too great to me. But I do want to be so "alive" to you that nothing else seems nearly as important. Let me honor you in my behavior at home, when playing with my friends, everywhere, and all the time. Let me be so alive in your love that nothing else matters. Amen.

THE HOLY SPIRIT
LIVES IN ME

The fruit of the Spirit is love, joy, peace,
forbearance, kindness, goodness, faithfulness,
gentleness and self-control.

Galatians 5:22–23

T he most beautiful work of the Holy Spirit is his ability
to put in me the qualities of Jesus.

The Holy Spirit in me grows the fruit of his patience,
his love, his peace, his self-control, and his faith. I don't
just look at how Jesus lived and try to imitate him.

Rather, I receive the Holy Spirit in me and learn how to
live by his power.

God, let all my thoughts and actions be transformed
by you; let my heart be filled with you. Fill me with the
Holy Spirit that all I do may be pleasing to you. Amen.

THE HOLY SPIRIT
WORKS IN ME

The entire law is fulfilled in keeping this one command:
"Love your neighbor as yourself."

Galatians 5:14

Jesus didn't just give me rules and regulations to obey. The Holy Spirit in me helps me love God with all my heart, soul, and mind, and helps me love others.

When I love God with everything in me, I always want to please him. Love like this obeys the law without needing any laws. The "law of love" is the highest law there is. When I live in love, I will do the right thing whether there is a law or not.

———

It pleases God when I love others. Today, I can pretend to wear a pair of glasses that helps me see everyone else the way God sees them. Then, whether they're mean or ugly or just ignore me, I can say to myself, "God, look at that beautiful person. You made them, and you love them just like you love me." It pleases God when I love others.

HOLY SPIRIT, LOVE IN ME

I pray that out of his glorious riches
he may strengthen you with power
through his Spirit in your inner being.

Ephesians 3:16

S ome of the teachings of Jesus seem difficult. He said, "love your enemies," "pray for those who hurt you," "turn the other cheek," and "walk a second mile."

Jesus' teachings are not a set of rules I need to obey. His teachings describe how I will live when the Holy Spirit is in control of my life. The power of the Holy Spirit in me makes the impossible possible!

Jesus, I can't honestly say I want to love my enemies, and I know I have a hard time praying for those who've hurt me. But I want to have the desire to do what you want me to do. Help me want to want to. I know, if you ask me to do something, I must be able to do it. You would never ask me to do something impossible. I just need to learn how to let you do it through me by the power of the Holy Spirit. Amen.

THE HOLY SPIRIT CHANGES ME

God's love has been poured out
into our hearts through the Holy Spirit,
who has been given to us.

Romans 5:5

I will give myself over completely to Jesus and let him rule over everything in my life. Then the Holy Spirit will pour God's love into me and help me be more like Jesus.

The more I let go of my own way of thinking and acting, the more he will help me think and act like Jesus. The more I empty myself of my sin and selfish ways, the more room he has to fill me with his love and power.

Dear God, be so at home in my heart that becoming like Jesus happens as naturally as taking my next breath. Remove from me anything that stands in the way of your will and fill me with the Holy Spirit. Teach me to be like Jesus. Amen.

OBEY FIRST

"Anyone who chooses to do the will of God
will find out whether my teaching comes from God
or whether I speak on my own."

John 7:17

The secret of understanding the teachings of Jesus is not curiosity, intelligence, or even determination. The secret is obedience.

If I have a desire in my heart to obey his words, I will begin to understand them. Obedience comes before understanding. The more I obey, the more I will understand.

———

I can imagine walking on a path in the woods on a dark night with a flashlight. The light shines just far enough, so I can see where to step. Then, when I step into the light that I have, the flashlight shines farther ahead, and I can see the next step. Jesus, help me to walk in the light of what I know about you so that, as I obey you, I get more "light" about what it means to follow your path. Amen.

TODAY IS IMPORTANT

I keep asking that the God of our Lord Jesus Christ,
the glorious Father, may give you the Spirit of wisdom
and revelation, so that you may know him better.

Ephesians 1:17

If I get too focused on the plan God has for my future,
I might miss out on enjoying God right now. The future
is now. God's plan is for me today, for this minute.

Getting to know him more and learning to trust him in
everything—past, present, and future—is God's plan for
me. If I focus on knowing God in the present, I will learn
how he thinks about my future.

--- --- ---

Dear God, give me a desire to live in your presence
today. And then tomorrow, the same all over again. I'm
just going to learn to enjoy your presence in the moment
and leave worrying about the future up to you. Amen.

QUESTIONS, QUESTIONS

I know whom I have believed,
and am convinced that he is able to guard
what I have entrusted to him.

2 Timothy 1:12

There will always be things about God that I will not be able to understand. If God could be fully known, he wouldn't be God.

I may suffer or see others I love suffer, and that might make me question God. Those are times I will have to go deeper in my knowledge of who he is. I still may not understand fully, but by trusting God, I will be given the strength and wisdom to handle anything that comes my way.

———

God, could you give me just enough strength to meet today's challenges? And just enough courage to face what I fear? And just enough wisdom to make good choices? And, God, if you give me all that today, then I don't have anything to fear. Amen.

ONLY GOD IS PERFECT

"I have called you friends,
for everything that I learned from my Father
I have made known to you."

John 15:15

The only friend who will never let me down is God. I may be hurt or disappointed by many other relationships. No human being can give me everything I need in a relationship. Humans are only human. When others fail me, I can learn to pray for them and treat them with kindness and love. After all, I disappoint my friends sometimes too.

God created me to be his friend. His friendship is the only one that will never fail me.

Dear God, you didn't have to create humans. You could have just created the world, flung it into the universe and set the orbit spinning. But you didn't. You created this wonder called life and gave all of us a chance to be friends with you. Help me, God, to never, never, ever take your friendship for granted. Amen.

LIKE A TREE,
STRAIGHT AND TALL

Whenever you face trials of any kind,
consider it nothing but joy, because you know that
the testing of your faith produces endurance; and
let endurance have its full effect, so that you may be
mature and complete, lacking in nothing.

James 1:2–4 NRSV

God is never finished with me! I will be growing in my relationship with him and my knowledge of his ways my entire life.

I will decide now, at this young age, to stick with God through thick and thin—good times and bad. I will always choose to ask him for the courage to stay faithful. That's how I will grow into the kind of person God created me to be.

God, keep my heart tender, my ears open, and my eyes on you, so I will always be willing to hear your voice and obey what I hear. Amen.

A TIME TO PRAY

After he had dismissed them,
he went up on a mountainside by himself to pray.
Later that night, he was there alone.

Matthew 14:23

Do I set aside a regular time each day to spend time with God? Sometimes prayer is just being quiet in God's presence. It's not asking for anything or saying anything, but just listening. It's hanging out with him.

God wants to make our "together time" the best part of my day.

Jesus, most of the time when I try to be quiet and just listen for your voice, I either fall asleep or hear only the endless chatter in my own head. But right now, I'm here. I want to know how to get quiet enough inside to hear your voice. Teach me, God, what it means to go "up on a mountainside by myself to pray," even if the mountainside is right here in my room. Amen.

WHY DO I HAVE TRIALS?

"I have told you these things, so that in me you
may have peace. In this world you will have trouble.
But take heart! I have overcome the world."

John 16:33

I can expect to have my share of troubles. God never
promises my life will be filled with only happy moments.
God uses the troubling times to make me strong in spirit.

God wants to go with me through any difficulty, so I will
learn to trust him and not myself.

God, I wish I could skip over troubling times and keep
only the happy times. I know life doesn't work that way,
but sometimes I wish it did. As I grow in faith and grow
as a person, make it clear to me what it means to trust
in you and not in myself. Amen.

A REASON
FOR EVERYTHING

I make known the end from the beginning . . .
I say, "My purpose will stand, and I will do
all that I please."

Isaiah 46:10

Because I don't always look at things the way God does,
I might miss God's purpose for my life.

Often I do not understand the reason for what I am
going through. But God knows. He is always working with
me, preparing me for something in the future.

I can always trust God's purpose for my life because he
sees from the beginning to the end. He can use everything
to mold me into the kind of person he wants me to be.

God, when I read a book, sometimes I like to peek at
the ending before I get to the end. Sometimes I wish
I could do that with life and see what's up ahead. But
then again, maybe that's not a good idea. Maybe that
would be like peeking at my Christmas presents before
Christmas. It might spoil the joy of being surprised.
God, when I want a sneak preview, help me trust in your
goodness. Amen.

GOD CAN
KEEP ME FULL

Has not God chosen those who are poor in the eyes
of the world to be rich in faith and to inherit the
kingdom he promised those who love him?

James 2:5

I may look at someone who is very talented and say,
"Wow, they would be a great Christian." In God's view,
how talented or smart a person is doesn't matter. What's
important to God is how dependent on him, or how "poor
in spirit," a person is.

The more aware I am of how dependent I am on God,
the more God can fill me with himself. That's called humility.

－－－－－

O God, empty me of myself like a cup of water poured
out on dry ground. Then fill me to the brim with the
Holy Spirit. Let the overflow of your life in me bless
those around me. Amen.

MY PURPOSE IN LIFE

I call to God, the Most High, to God,
who supplies my every need.

Psalm 57:2 GNB

God has one main purpose for my life: that I should be his friend.

I will never understand what God is doing in my life unless I keep in a close relationship with him. If I make it my purpose to know God and have a close friendship with him, I will see that he can use everything that happens to me for my good.

— — — —

God, draw me ever closer to you. Fill me, mold me, and shape me so I can fit into your purposes for my life. Today, draw me even closer to you. Amen.

LETTING GOD ANSWER HIS WAY

I tried to think this problem through,
but it was too difficult for me until I went
into your Temple. Then I understood.

Psalm 73:16–17 GNB

If I pray just to get answers, I will get angry with God. The answers will come eventually, but often not in the way I expect and not on my timetable. The reason for prayer is to get close enough to God so I begin to understand *why* he answers the way he does.

The main purpose of prayer is not to get the answers but to know God.

———

God, praying for the things I want is so much easier than praying to know you. You seem so unknowable! I know you sent Jesus to show me what you are like, and that tells me how much you love me. Today, God, I pray for the understanding I need to know you even though there are things I don't understand about you. Amen.

I TALK TO
MY BEST FRIEND

Rejoice always, pray continually,
give thanks in all circumstances;
for this is God's will for you in Christ Jesus.

1 Thessalonians 5:16–18

A m I always in contact with God, or do I pray only
when I'm in trouble or when things are going wrong?

Learning to live every minute of every day in the
presence of God means talking things over with him all day
long and listening.

That's what best friends do when they walk together.

––––––

Today, God, help me imagine Jesus is going everywhere
with me. Actually, that's not just my imagination. That's
the truth! He is always beside me. Help me learn to be
aware of that truth every day, all day long. Amen.

I TALK TO MY FATHER

Because you are children,
God has sent the Spirit of his Son into
our hearts, crying, "Abba Father!"

Galatians 4:6 NRSV

When God put his Spirit in me, I became his child, his dearest son or daughter.

As a child of God, I can exercise the special privilege of a child, the privilege of always being face-to-face with my heavenly Father. That is the true meaning of prayer: talking with God just like I chat with my earthly father (or grandfather).

"Abba" is the most intimate word for father in the language Jesus spoke. It's like me saying, "dearest Daddy!" Abba is the name the Holy Spirit gives us for God.

I can hardly believe that I can use a word like that for the God of the universe, but that's exactly what Jesus said to do. Today, I'll practice calling God Abba every time I think of him. I think he'd like that.

GOD LIKES TO VISIT

Surely the arm of the LORD is not too short to save,
nor his ear too dull to hear.

Isaiah 59:1

As a child of God I can be certain that my heavenly
Father always hears my prayers.

As God's child, my prayers will never be ignored. I will
never be turned away by my heavenly Father when I want
to talk with him.

God is never too busy to listen. His door is always open.

———

God, what about kids who don't have fathers? Or kids
whose dads are mean? How can they understand that
they have a loving heavenly father? God, today I pray
for all the kids who don't have loving dads. I don't
understand why every kid can't have a warm, loving,
and safe home. Somehow, God, make it okay for kids
who don't. And if I can help make it a little better for
another kid today, show me what you want me to do.
Amen.

PRAYING IN
TROUBLED TIMES

We also boast of our troubles,
because we know that trouble produces
endurance, endurance brings God's approval, and his
approval creates hope. This hope does not disappoint
us, for God has poured out his love into our hearts
by means of the Holy Spirit, who is God's gift to us.

Romans 5:3–5

When I am going through a difficult time, feeling sorry
for myself won't help.

Instead, I can go to my heavenly Father and tell him all
my feelings, both the good and bad.

I know he will bring me through any difficulty and use
it to make me more like Jesus.

Thank you, God, for being with me in everything,
especially the tough times. Thank you for trusting me
with trials. Have your way in my life, and use every
difficulty to teach me to trust you even more. Amen.

GROWING UP WITH GOD

"I will be a Father to you, and you will be my sons
and daughters," says the Lord Almighty.

2 Corinthians 6:18

I may have become a child of God through my parents'
influence and that's wonderful. But as I grow up, I will
want to learn to trust God in my own way.

The stronger my personal relationship with my
heavenly Father grows, the more I will begin to influence
others with my faith.

I will never forget that no matter how young or old I am,
God will always be my Father, and I will always be his child.

God, thank you so much for those who love and care for
me, especially my parents, grandparents, and teachers.
Thank you that I'm in a home with a family that cares
about whether or not I want to live my life for you. Help
me to be a good son or daughter for my parents. But
especially help me be a son or daughter who brings joy
to my heavenly Father. Amen.

STRONG IN GOD'S STRENGTH

"Be strong and courageous.
Do not be afraid; do not be discouraged,
for the Lord your God will be with you wherever you go."

Joshua 1:9

I find out how much I trust God when trouble comes into my life.

If I have really been learning to trust him, I can go through almost anything and not lose my confidence in his strength to get me through it.

I bring great joy to God's heart when I endure difficult trials with courage, and remain faithful to him.

God, no matter where my life leads, what I grow up to be, or how tough things might be, I want to be strong and courageous. I not only ask you to give me strength, I want you to be my strength. Teach me how to let you be my strength, even when I feel weak. Amen.

GOD'S QUIET VOICE

"The LORD, your God, is in your midst,
a warrior who gives victory; he will rejoice over
you with gladness, he will renew you in his love;
he will exult over you with loud singing."

Zephaniah 3:17 NRSV

In any difficulty I experience, there is always something in me that God wants to improve on. He may want to work on my attitude or my relationship with him.

The only way I will know God's purpose is to be very quiet before him. God often speaks in a voice so gentle that I can miss it if I am not quiet.

I want to learn to shut out the noise and the distractions around me, enter into his presence, and wait with a thankful heart. He will show me what he's up to if I wait on him.

— — — — —

God, I'm not very good at shutting out the noise around me. Silence can feel kind of weird. God, help me learn to create quiet moments for us to hang out together. Could you help me think of a quiet spot or time of day that can be our special meeting place? Amen.

GOD DISCIPLINES IN LOVE

Endure trials for the sake of discipline.
God is treating you as children; for what child is there
whom a parent does not discipline?

Hebrews 12:7 NRSV

As a child of God, I may be disciplined by my heavenly Father.

He disciplines me because he loves me and wants me to line up with his purposes for my life. Sometimes God uses a difficult time to discipline me. Or sometimes, the consequences of my bad behavior can be a form of discipline. When that happens, I need to let him have his way with me and bring me back into line.

God loves me too much to just leave me alone!

— — — — —

God, bring it on! If I'm off track, sidetracked, or if I lose sight of the track altogether, do whatever you have to do to get me back on track with your will. I don't want to miss out on any of the plans you have for me. Amen.

SIGNS OF
A TRUE DISCIPLE

Grow in the grace and knowledge
of our Lord and Savior Jesus Christ.

2 Peter 3:18

There are several signs that I have been born again by the Spirit of God.

First, I become sensitive to sin and the need to immediately confess and turn from it.

Second, my understanding and knowledge of who Jesus is begins to deepen, and our friendship becomes more meaningful.

Third, I will begin to have a much clearer picture of God's purpose for my life.

Are these signs present in my life?

– – – – –

God, I want to grow in grace and knowledge of you. How that happens and when that happens, I'm not totally sure about. I'll leave that in your hands. I just know I want to live my life for you. Amen.

KNOWING
JESUS PERSONALLY

"The Holy Spirit, whom the Father will send in my
name, will teach you all things and will remind you
of everything I have said to you."

John 14:26

I t is possible to know the words and teachings of the
New Testament and not know Jesus personally.

In fact, it is only when I invite the Holy Spirit into my
heart that I can understand the words Jesus spoke. The
main job of the Holy Spirit is to apply what Jesus taught to
my everyday life.

— — — —

Come, Holy Spirit; come! Live in my heart, bring
understanding to my mind, and teach me how to live
according to the ways Jesus taught. Amen.

WHAT'S BEST ISN'T ALWAYS EASY

"Love your enemies,
do good to those who hate you,
bless those who curse you,
pray for those who mistreat you."

Luke 6:27–28

Following Jesus is not always an easy life. Jesus asks us to do hard things.

He asks us to love our enemies and even pray for those who are mean to us. He asks us to put him ahead of everything else, even our parents. He asks us to follow him even if it means suffering and persecution.

Am I ready to follow Jesus, knowing it will be hard?

———

Jesus, I think I'm ready to say yes to whatever you ask of me, at least I want to say yes. When it's hard for me to do the right thing, please give me the strength to follow you. Give me the desire to say yes to you. Amen.

I'LL STICK WITH IT

"Whoever does not carry their cross
and follow me cannot be my disciple."

Luke 14:27

If I want to follow Jesus but change my mind when the going gets tough, my life will not be very satisfying. I can decide now: "I am going to stick with Jesus no matter how hard it gets." Then I will have a deep joy no one can ever take away.

Following Jesus doesn't mean everything will go right. And it doesn't guarantee happiness, health, or success. But following Jesus does mean I can know a deep, inner joy and peace no matter what happens around me.

— — — —

I think I'll ask some older people who have gone through a hard time and are still living a godly life how they did it. I bet they have some secrets they could share with me.

BE HONEST, BE OPEN

God is light; in him there is no darkness at all . . .
if we walk in the light, as he is in the light, we have
fellowship with one another, and the blood of Jesus,
his Son, purifies us from all sin.

1 John 1:5, 7

Nothing is more important than keeping an open relationship with God.

If there is anything coming between me and God, I will talk with him about it right now. I will bring it into the light. I won't ignore it.

It won't go away by itself. I must deal with it now. I will do it right now!

- - - - -

Lord, I don't want anything to separate me from you. If there is anything in my life, anything I'm doing or any way I'm thinking that displeases you, show me so I can be done with it. Let nothing distract me or blind me to your love. Be Lord of my life today and every day. Amen.

LEAVE OTHERS UP TO GOD

"Blessed are you when people insult you,
persecute you and falsely say all kinds of evil
against you because of me."

Matthew 5:11

Jesus tells me to pray for others even when they misunderstand me, mistreat me, or are mean to me.

By praying for them and then leaving them in God's care, God will use even their hurtful actions to draw me closer to him.

Plus, keeping a loving attitude toward others when they mistreat me might make them want to know God like I do.

— — — —

God, I can learn to pray for my teacher even if she embarrasses me in class. I can pray for my friend who ditched me to play with someone else. Or if someone yells at me and blames me for something I didn't do, I can still pray for that person. Sometimes people do mean things because they're tired or stressed out. I know I do. Help me to love them anyway and to pray they'll feel your love. Amen.

THE STRANGE SECRET

The foolishness of God is wiser than
human wisdom, and the weakness of God
is stronger than human strength.

1 Corinthians 1:25

The strange secret of the kingdom of God is that when I feel weak that is when I am strong.

When I am feeling confident in myself, it is hard for me to depend on God. It is far better for me to recognize my own weakness and tap into God's power.

His power is always greater than my puny strength.

God, I don't usually feel confident that I can be a good follower of Jesus. A lot of times I don't even feel very loving or kind. So, God, make me strong in my weakness, wise in my foolishness, and loving in my self-centeredness. Show me how to depend on you and tap into your strength. God, be my strength. Amen.

GOD'S POWER IN ME

"I baptize you with water, but he [Jesus]
will baptize you with the Holy Spirit."

Mark 1:8

Jesus wants to baptize me with the Holy Spirit. He wants to completely cover me, drench me, and soak me with the power of the Holy Spirit. Then I can learn to do everything by his power and not my own strength.

The only way I can live like God plans for me to live is to have the power of his Spirit inside me and all over me.

- - - - -

To be baptized means to be immersed or drenched. If I fell into the lake with all my clothes on, I would be completely soaked with water. That's a picture of what Jesus wants to do for me. He wants to completely cover me (baptize me) with the Holy Spirit. Then I will have the power to show others how great he is. "Lord Jesus, baptize me with the Holy Spirit. Amen."

A TIME AND PLACE TO PRAY

"When you pray, go into your room,
close the door and pray to your Father, who is unseen.
Then your Father, who sees what is done
in secret, will reward you."

Matthew 6:6

I t is important to have a special time and place where I can pray. Prayer takes self-discipline. I have to shut out other things to concentrate in prayer. If I can get into the habit of "closing the door" on all distractions and focus on God sometime during each day, I know he will become more dear to me than anything or anyone else.

Discipline means doing what I need to do, whether I feel like it or not.

It takes discipline to learn to do anything well. It doesn't matter whether it's learning to play a musical instrument, improving in a sport, or learning what it means to follow Jesus. It all takes practice, or discipline. Prayer is a discipline. The more I practice being in the presence of God, the more natural it will become for me. The reward for prayer is a deeper knowledge of God and his love.

CONFESS, THEN PRAY

"Who can stand in the presence of the LORD,
this holy God?"

1 Samuel 6:20

The first step to take in prayer is to confess any sin that is coming between me and God.

He loves me too much to let me hang on to anything that can separate me from his presence. The way into the presence of God always goes through the door marked "confession."

— — — —

God, create in me a clean heart and renew a right spirit within me. I confess the things I've done and the things I've left undone that are displeasing to you. Forgive me, O God, and draw me close to you today. Amen.

DEEP LOVE

How I love to do your will, my God!
I keep your teaching in my heart.

Psalm 40:8 GNB

When I am filled with the Holy Spirit, serving God and doing his will is a joy.

The Holy Spirit gives me such a deep love for Jesus that I would give up anything, even life itself, to please him. I always get great joy when I please someone I love deeply.

———————

Jesus, let my love for you be so strong that being my best for you is the most important thing in my life. Be everything to me. Teach me how to put you ahead of every other thing or person. You gave everything for me; I want to give everything to you. Amen.

DEEP PEACE

"Peace I leave with you; my peace I give you.
I do not give to you as the world gives. Do not let
your hearts be troubled and do not be afraid."

John 14:27

Jesus said, "My peace I leave with you."
Jesus had peace in the middle of deep suffering and trials because he had a perfect relationship with his Father. There was nothing in his life that separated him from God.

The peace I have as a child of God—the peace Jesus gives—is based on my friendship with my heavenly Father. Peace isn't based on what's happening around me. I can be completely peaceful when I'm trusting him.

- - - - -

Jesus, I don't feel very peaceful a lot of times. Teach me how to have the kind of peace you had. You had the peace that comes from a completely open and honest relationship with your heavenly Father. When I'm worried, stressed, fearful, or upset, help me to be open and honest with you about it. Then I can experience the kind of peace you had. Amen.

WALK WHERE THERE IS LIGHT

God is light;
in him there is no darkness at all.

1 John 1:5

"**W**alking in the light" means being in the bright light of the presence of God.

When I walk in the light, the light shines on anything in me that is not pleasing to God. Will I choose to step into that light every day? Or will I hide things in the dark that I don't want God to see? Will I let God expose any secret or hidden thought or action that might be separating me from him?

––––––

If I confess my sins (that means telling God what I've done and how I feel about anything I've done wrong), God will forgive me. Sometimes I need to ask the person I hurt to forgive me; sometimes I need to ask God to help me forgive myself. But all I have to do is ask. Then God promises to forgive me, to make me clean on the inside, and make right my relationship with him and with others.

PRAYER IS LIKE FOOD

"Lord, teach us to pray."

Luke 11:1

When I was born again by the Spirit of God, God put his life in me. Now I need to feed and care for that life.

I feed my physical body by eating healthy food. I can feed the life of God in me too. I can fill my inner being with healthy practices like prayer, study, meditating, and serving others.

The choice I have is to either starve his life in me or to feed it. How well am I caring for the life of God in me?

– – – – –

My dad and mom would never think of starving me. Besides, they are responsible for caring for me. They don't care for me because they have to. They do it because they love me. I want to be responsible for the care and feeding of God's life in me. That is a serious responsibility, but love causes me to take on serious tasks with great enthusiasm.

MAKING
WEAK FAITH STRONG

Fight the good fight of the faith.

1 Timothy 6:12

C ommon sense is not faith. Faith is much more than that. Faith is supernatural; it is above and beyond my natural abilities. My faith must be stretched to grow. The stretching will usually come in the form of difficulties in my life.

Is there a problem in my life I have a hard time believing God can solve? If I choose to keep my confidence in God, then every test will only make my faith stronger. My faith grows the most when I fight through difficulties and doubts and keep trusting God.

God, I know I complain sometimes about certain problems. But I really want you to stretch me to make my faith grow. Let my confidence always be in you, not in my own abilities to solve every problem that comes along. Teach me to trust you. Amen.

GOD WILL USE ME

"Out of the believer's heart shall flow rivers of living
water." Now he said this about the Spirit,
which believers in him were to receive.

John 7:38–39 NRSV

I f I want to be used by God, I will always try to keep my
relationship right with him.

If I will do that, he will make my life like a river of living
water to those around me. I will refresh them and bless
them. The blessings don't happen because of who I am but
because the Holy Spirit is flowing through me.

God, today, wherever I am and whoever I meet, I can
be a blessing. The Holy Spirit in me wants to flow onto
other people and refresh them like a cold drink of water
on a hot day. Let nothing in my life today block the flow
of the Holy Spirit's blessing. Amen.

DEEP JOY

"Remain in my love . . .
that your joy may be complete."

John 15:10–11

The source of real joy is not good health, popularity, or success. Nor is it the result of any circumstance or event. Real joy comes from knowing God and having the kind of relationship with him that Jesus himself had. Jesus had an "all I have is yours, and all you have is mine" kind of relationship with his heavenly Father.

I want God to show me how to be that close to him. I want to be so close that we share everything.

God, let me find my joy in the fact that I have a right relationship with you and that you love me and I love to please you. I never want to look anywhere else for joy. Put such a deep joy in me that, no matter what happens, I can still be happy and have a good attitude. Amen.

SEPTEMBER

CLEAN INSIDE

Make every effort to live in peace
with everyone and to be holy.

Hebrews 12:14

It would be a good idea to remind myself every day what the purpose of my life is.

It is not happiness or health; it's holiness. Holiness means to be completely devoted to God and God alone and to be set apart for God's use.

Do I really believe it's possible to be entirely dedicated to God? If that is God's purpose for me, I have to believe he can help me do it. God, show me what it really means for me to be holy.

— — — —

God, what does it mean to be holy? I don't think it means I have to be serious all the time or can't have any fun. After all, Jesus went to weddings and parties and loved being with people. If Jesus wasn't fun to be around, I don't think so many people would have followed him everywhere. God, make me the kind of holy like Jesus was so that others want to hang around with you too. Amen.

JESUS INSIDE

You were taught . . . to be made new in the attitude
of your minds; and to put on the new self, created to be
like God in true righteousness and holiness.

Ephesians 4:22–24

To be holy means to let God make me like his Son
Jesus. It will not happen instantly. As I let go of all
behaviors, attitudes, and thoughts that are not Christ-like,
the Holy Spirit will teach me how to be like Jesus.

The same Spirit that was in Jesus is in me. He wants to
make me like Jesus. He wants to make me holy. Holy Spirit,
help me cooperate!

— — — — —

Jesus, make me the kind of holy that treats others with
compassion. Make me the kind of holy that stands up
against what is wrong and seeks to do what is right.
Make me the kind of holy that cares about those who
are hungry or cold or have no home. And most of all,
God, make me the kind of holy that is filled with your
love. Amen.

MAKE ME A BLESSING

May God himself, the God of peace,
sanctify you through and through.
May your whole spirit, soul and body be
kept blameless at the coming
of our Lord Jesus Christ.

1 Thessalonians 5:23

To be holy means to be set apart for God's use, and to be sanctified. Sanctified means that I use everything God has given me to be my best for him.

Have I determined that everything I am—all my abilities, talents, and gifts—will be dedicated to God's service?

God gave me all those things. Only as I offer them back to him for his use can he make my life a blessing to others.

God, I do want to be set apart for your use, and sanctified. I want to use all my talents to bring honor to you. Let my life be a blessing to others. Let my life make a difference for you. Amen.

I'M GOD'S PROPERTY

If we live, we live for the Lord; and if we die,
we die for the Lord. So, whether we live or die,
we belong to the Lord.

Romans 14:8

When I give myself to God, I become God's possession. God becomes responsible for me. And since I belong to God, I can trust him to bring me through everything that comes into my life. No matter what happens, good or bad or easy or difficult, I can trust God.

Because I belong to God, I will never have to worry about my life again. He will take care of me.

- - - - -

Thank you, God, that my life is in your care and that I belong to you. Help me to always remember who I belong to, and help me live like that's really true. I want to be wholly yours forever. Amen.

I'LL BE
A GOOD LISTENER

"Blessed is the one whom God corrects;
so do not despise the discipline of the Almighty."

Job 5:17

It is perfectly natural for me to ask God questions when I am having a difficult time. But we never need to question whether God is good or not.

He has a purpose in everything, especially when bringing me through any trial. Sometimes I just won't be able to understand what possible good can come from a difficult situation. Then I can just ask God to teach me what I can learn from what I'm going through.

- - - - -

God, when I'm having a really lousy day, help me remember to ask, "Father, what are you trying to teach me in this?" Maybe if I began to ask that, my lousy days would turn into days I could actually be thankful for. So, God, help me remember to ask and to be open to your answer. Amen.

A RIVER OF BLESSING

Happy are those who reject the advice
of evil people, who do not follow the example
of sinners or join those who have no use for God.
Instead, they find joy in obeying the Law of the
LORD, and they study it day and night.

Psalm 1:1–2 GNB

Jesus not only sent the Holy Spirit to live *in* me but also to flow *out* of me to bless others.

Am I letting the Holy Spirit flow out of me? Or am I allowing things into my life that block the flow of that blessing?

Is it a joy to obey God? Do I meditate on his Word throughout the day and at night? Am I cooperating with the Holy Spirit, so he can keep me in the presence of God? I will confess my shortcomings today and every day and ask the Holy Spirit to fill me. Then the stream of God's Spirit will flow out of me freely to bless others.

God, I want to be filled with the Holy Spirit today and every day. Show me anything in my life that is blocking the flow of your life out of me. Help me to be sensitive to doing or saying anything that would keep you from blessing others through me. Fill me right now, Holy Spirit. Amen.

MORE AND MORE OF JESUS

The disciples were filled with joy
and with the Holy Spirit.

Acts 13:52

The Holy Spirit in me is the source of blessing for others. The Holy Spirit is the Spirit of Jesus. As long as I continue to be filled with his Spirit, the more qualities that are like Jesus—kindness, forgiveness, and love— will flow out to those around me.

I want to be sure nothing is keeping me from always being filled with the Holy Spirit. And I want to be sure nothing is stopping him from flowing out of me to bless others.

O God, let me live this day full of your Spirit. Let all my thoughts and actions reflect the truth that you are living inside me. Let me be sensitive to any behavior or attitude that is preventing me from being a blessing to others. Amen.

GOD'S WAY
IS ALWAYS BEST

Let endurance have its full effect,
so that you may be mature and complete,
lacking in nothing.

James 1:4

Once I have been born again, I will enter into a battle. The battle is to choose to follow God's will every day instead of following my own way. I will be tempted daily to please myself and fulfill my own desires.

If I consistently choose God, these choices will turn into good habits. Good habits eventually produce Christ-like character in me.

– – – – –

God, take my life and shape my will according to your ways. When selfishness creeps in and I find myself insisting on wanting my own way, forgive me. Renew in me a willingness to serve you at home, at school, or at play and in all my thoughts and actions. Amen.

GOOD HABITS

A heart at peace gives life
to the body, but envy rots the bones.
Proverbs 14:30

I want to get into the habit, right now, of asking my heavenly Father to show me his will about the choices I make.

He will give me a calm and peaceful spirit about the right choices. When I am thinking about making a bad choice, I will feel uncomfortable inside.

When I ask God to guide me and am willing to wait for his direction, I can make the right choices. I want to learn to wait for the peace of God in my heart. I don't want to run ahead of God. I don't want to do things that make me feel uncomfortable inside.

— — — — —

God, sometimes I wish you would be clearer about what you want me to do. Waiting for a peaceful heart seems like waiting for the medicine to work when I have a fever. Both take time. I never want to run ahead of you. Help me learn to be patient. Amen.

GOD SEES EVERYTHING

The prayer of a righteous person
is powerful and effective.

James 5:16

Prayer is the main practice that will make me strong
spiritually. Another way to spend my alone time with
God is worshiping him. Worship is simply thanking God for
who he is and what he has done for me. It is also telling
him how much I love him and want to serve him. It is
allowing him to tell me how much he loves me.

If I can learn to be faithful in this part of my life—the
part that no one else sees—God will be able to use me in
ways I can't even imagine right now.

God, I think remembering to pray is the hardest part of
praying. I get busy or tired. Or I play so hard that when
it's time to go to bed, all I want to do is go to sleep.
God, keep me mindful of you. In the midst of being an
ordinary kid doing ordinary kid things, keep me mindful
of you. God, even when I forget to pray, I still give you
my life, my play, my today, and all my tomorrows. Amen.

SIMPLE THINGS, RIGHT ATTITUDES

"You have been faithful with a few things;
I will put you in charge of many things."

Matthew 25:23

Jesus performed one of the most common, ordinary tasks in his culture: he washed his disciples' feet. He said we should do the same kinds of things.

What common and ordinary tasks might I be required to do? My attitude while doing them says a lot about how serious I am about being like Jesus. It takes God's power to do simple things with a Christ-like attitude.

God, I don't like to clean my room or make my bed. I stall when my mom asks me to help with dinner. I put off doing homework. My attitude when doing the ordinary things I'm supposed to do is not always that great. Forgive me, God, for being resentful when I'm asked to do something at home. And forgive me for putting off things I know I'm supposed to do. Create in me a Christ-like spirit, so that in doing ordinary, everyday things, I can be faithful to you. Amen.

I CAN PRAY ANYTIME

Be still before the LORD
and wait patiently for him.

Psalm 37:7

There will be times when I will not feel like praying. Other times, I may wonder if it will do any good to pray. I will pray anyway!

My heavenly Father will always answer. Sometimes the answer is yes, and sometimes it's no. Other times he will say, "Wait!" because he wants me to learn something. While I'm waiting, he has the time to teach me things I might not have learned if he had said yes right away.

– – – – –

God, I'm not good at waiting. When I pray, I want answers! But, God, if your answers were like push-button responses to my prayers, I would be in control, not you. So, God, be with me through the "waiting" times as well as the "action" times. Teach me when to act and when to wait. Amen.

SAY "NO!"
TO BEING SELFISH

Commit to the Lord whatever you do,
and he will establish your plans.

Proverbs 16:3

Jesus asks me not to insist on having my own way and to surrender to God's will and ways.

The reason God gently asks me to surrender to him is because I do not always know what is best for me. When I do surrender, I never need to worry about how things will work out.

God is able to care for everything.

———

God, I want to learn to live for you every day. Surrender means to give up and give away power or control. God, today I'm waving a white flag and surrendering everything to you. Keep my heart fully yielded to you. Help me to remember who's in control. Amen.

DON'T BE CONFUSED

You keep him in perfect peace whose mind
is stayed on you, because he trusts in you.

Isaiah 26:3 ESV

If I will always be honest with God about what's going on
in my life, I will continually grow in my understanding of
God's will for my life. But if I start to hide things from him
and go my own way, there will be confusion.

Obeying God in the smallest details is how I will learn
to know his will for my life.

- - - - -

God, my mind is rarely "stayed on you." Most days I let
big things and little things keep me from thinking about
you. Sometimes it's worrying about something or just
being afraid. Or I might be distracted by everything
going on around me. God, help me stay focused on you,
and keep me rooted and grounded in your love. Amen.

FOLLOW GOD, NOT OTHERS

We are not trying to please people but God,
who tests our hearts.

1 Thessalonians 2:4

"**E**verybody else is doing it" is not the standard for my life. Doing something just because my friends are doing it is not being my best for God. God has a higher standard for me.

Have I chosen to dedicate everything I am—all my abilities, talents, and gifts—to God? God gave me all those things. Only as I give them back to him will I make decisions according to the highest standard. The highest standard is being my best for God.

———

As I think back through the past twenty-four hours, I'll picture myself in a play. The stage is where I was that day: at home, school, or playing with a friend. I'll imagine Jesus sitting in the audience. What was I doing in the morning? Who was I with at lunch? How about outside? As I remember my day, was there a smile on Jesus' face? Was Jesus happy with my choices and the words that I spoke? Is there something I need to confess? I pray that I will not act or think in any manner which would not be pleasing to Jesus.

FIND A SPECIAL PLACE
TO PRAY

One of those days Jesus went out to a mountainside
to pray, and spent the night praying to God.

Luke 6:12

The secret to learning how to pray is simply to begin
praying.

I will want to find a place to pray where no one will
interrupt me or even know I am praying. It will be a place
where I can shut out distractions and be alone with God.
I will choose a place and time where my main motive is to
get to know my Father in heaven.

Living as a follower of Jesus will be impossible without
definite times of private prayer.

— — — —

God, teach me how to pray. Teach me how to make
prayer as much a part of my life as breathing. Teach me,
O God, how to live in your presence all the time and not
only when I'm alone with you in prayer. Amen.

SAY "NO!" TO TEMPTATION

God is faithful; he will not let you be tempted beyond
what you can bear. But when you are tempted, he will
also provide a way out so that you can endure it.

1 Corinthians 10:13

Temptation is not sin. Temptation is something I must
face if I am to grow in Christ. I cannot escape facing it,
but I can escape giving in to it.

God gives me the power, in the middle of temptation,
to escape if I will make that choice.

God, every day I'm tempted to do something I know I
shouldn't. Tell a lie. Say something bad about someone.
Make fun of someone. Sometimes I might even be
tempted to take something that's not mine. Forgive me,
God, when temptations to do wrong are stronger than
my desire to do right. Amen.

SATAN IS A TEMPTER

Be alert, be on watch! Your enemy, the Devil,
roams around like a roaring lion,
looking for someone to devour.
Be firm in your faith and resist him . . .

1 Peter 5:8–9 GNB

As a child of God, with the Holy Spirit living in me,
Satan will tempt me with all sorts of lies: I'm not good
enough; nobody likes me; God doesn't care about me; or
one little white lie won't hurt.

I need to learn to resist Satan the minute he attacks
me with one of his lies. When I resist him and ask for God's
help, he will flee.

Jesus, fill my day with the light of your love. Help me
resist the temptation of the enemy. Fill my thoughts
with your truth that I may be my best for you. Amen.

SATAN IS A LIAR

"When he [the devil] lies, he speaks his native language, for he is a liar and the father of lies."

John 8:44

Satan will most often tempt me to go the way of the crowd. The devil will tell me: "It's too hard to follow Jesus." He'll say, "It will cost you too much to be his disciple." Or he will try to convince me: "Just be like everybody else."

Will I resist Satan's temptations to follow the ways of the world? Will I fix my eyes on Jesus and remain loyal to him no matter the cost?

———

Jesus, sometimes I just want to do what everyone else is doing. When I'm not sure if it's the right thing to do, give me the strength to stop. Help me see clearly what being my best for you looks like in everyday situations. Fix my eyes on you, even when I'm distracted by what everyone else is doing around me. Amen.

LIVING A LIFE
THAT WINS

"Be perfect, therefore,
as your heavenly Father is perfect."

Matthew 5:48

Following Jesus is not a matter of just trying to act a certain way. It's not a performance.

It is letting God change me on the inside—in my heart—so that my natural actions are pleasing to him.

The Holy Spirit can empower me to line my actions up perfectly with how God wants me to live.

God, I'm not sure I know what "be perfect" means. I know I'm not perfect and am far from it! So I'm thinking that what you mean by "be perfect" is that you and I have a "perfect" relationship. That I'm not hiding anything from you. That there's nothing we can't talk over. That my heart is completely open to you, and I am willing to do whatever you ask of me. God, I want my heart to be perfectly open to you, so you can shape me into the person you want me to be. Amen.

ENJOYING GOD EVERY DAY

We pray . . . that the name of our Lord Jesus may
be glorified in you, and you in him, according to
the grace of our God and the Lord Jesus Christ.

2 Thessalonians 1:12

The whole human race was created to glorify God and
enjoy him forever.

Sin has switched the human race to another track,
but it has not changed God's purpose at all.

When I am born again, I discover his great purpose for
me: I am created for God, and I get to be on his track for life.

————

God, I give myself to you—all of me—when I'm good
and when I'm not so good. When I'm honest and when
I'm tricky. When I'm loving and when I'm selfish. Take
me and make me in your image. Fill me with the Holy
Spirit. Amen.

JESUS SEES MY HEART

Those who make themselves clean from all those
evil things, will be used for special purposes,
because they are dedicated and useful to
their Master, ready to be used for every good deed.

2 Timothy 2:21 GNB

When I call Jesus "Master," I am saying, "You know me better than I know myself. You understand my deepest desires. You know what's best for me. I will obey you without question."

Can I really call Jesus "Master"?

- - - -

Jesus, I want to call you "Master" . . . sometimes. But other times? Not so much. Jesus, create in me the desire to call you my Lord and Master and live like I really mean it. And make me noble, holy, and useful in your kingdom. I know those desires will have come from you, because they won't come from me! Lord, cleanse my heart. Amen.

JESUS, MY MASTER

"I have set you an example that you should
do as I have done for you. Very truly, I tell you,
servants are not greater than their master."

John 13:15–16 NRSV

If I call Jesus my Master, that means I have decided to follow and obey him no matter what happens.

Friends may turn against me. My family could misunderstand me. But even if I get discouraged, I will still follow my Master.

Jesus, be Lord of my life and master of my heart's desires, even now when I'm a kid. And prepare me for the work you would have me do. Make me a "kingdom kid." Amen.

GOD'S SEARCHLIGHT

Create in me a clean heart, O God,
and put a new and right spirit within me.

Psalm 51:10 NRSV

Do I have anything I want to hide from God? I will be as honest as I can be. I will let God search me with his light.

When his light reveals anything I might be trying to hide from him, I will confess it. I won't ignore it even if it is a tiny thing.

Behind that tiny thing is a big sin, an attitude that says, "I will not do what God says; I will do what I want to do." Every day I want to keep open and honest with God and let his light reveal anything that separates me from his presence.

––– –––

Keep my heart pure, O God, so I can walk in your light and be forgiven, loved, and guided every moment of this day. Amen.

THE IMPOSSIBLE IS POSSIBLE

"And whoever does not carry their cross
and follow me cannot be my disciple. ...
In the same way, those of you who do not
give up everything you have cannot be my disciples."

Luke 14:27, 33

C alling Jesus master requires supernatural power.
God doesn't ask me just to do what comes easily and
naturally. He asks me to do what he has equipped me to do
by the power of his Spirit working in me.

That is what being his follower means. It means that
I can do, through God's power in me, what I cannot do with
my own power.

— — — —

Jesus, I'm willing to be your servant. I want to do your
will. You have incredible, awesome supernatural power.
You demonstrated that when you rose from the dead. Do
through me what I can't do on my own, in big ways and
little ways, today and every day. Amen.

WHO DO I
NEED TO SEE?

"If you are offering your gift at the altar
and there remember that your brother or sister
has something against you, leave your gift there
in front of the altar. First go and be reconciled to them;
then come and offer your gift."

Matthew 5:23–24

Since I am a follower of Jesus, when a person is mean to me, I will not wait until they ask for my forgiveness. I will humbly go to them and offer to clear up anything that has come between us.

Jesus cares more about my relationships than about who's right and who's wrong.

— — — —

Jesus, is it more important to me to "be right" than to do the right thing? Is there anyone I need to make things right with? Keep me honest with myself and with you. Show me if there is anyone with whom I need to make things right. Forgive me when I fail to honor you in my relationships. Amen.

I'LL BE LOYAL

Let us not grow weary in doing what is right,
for we will reap at harvest time, if we do not give up.

Galatians 6:9 NRSV

After deciding to follow Jesus, my loyalty to him will be tested. Some of my friends will want me to turn away from him and follow the crowd. I will go through trials that test my faith.

I will pray daily for God's strength to help me stay true. I will not grow weary in doing what is right.

Jesus says, "You are my friends if you do what I command." Spending time getting to know Jesus is the only way I can become friends with him. I learn who Jesus is by learning how to pray, reading the Bible, and spending quiet time with him. I don't do those things to make God love me more because he couldn't love me more than he already does. I do those things to get to know his Son, Jesus.

WHO'S MOST IMPORTANT?

"No one who puts a hand to the plow
and looks back is fit for service
in the kingdom of God."

Luke 9:62

Jesus wants me to place so much importance on our relationship that it is as if no other relationship matters. Do I have any other relationships that are more important to me than Jesus?

I don't want anyone or anything to keep me from moving into the future God has for me. I want to keep moving forward with God and never look back!

— — — —

God, if I'm honest, I have to admit a lot of relationships might be more important to me than Jesus. It's hard for me to imagine how to make Jesus more important than my dad and mom or my brothers and sisters. I know I have a lot of growing up to do. Help me understand more and more how to put my relationship with you first. Amen.

I'LL TELL THE GOOD NEWS

I am not ashamed of the gospel,
because it is the power of God that brings salvation
to everyone who believes.

Romans 1:16

God may not call me to be a preacher, but he does call me to preach the gospel. Every disciple of Jesus has a privilege of telling others about the good news of salvation.

For every follower of Jesus, the purpose of life is to know God. The mission in life is to make him known to others. As I learn to know Jesus more and more, I will want others to know him as well.

Lord Jesus, help me to live in such a way that others who meet me will want to know you better. Teach me how to tell others about you, whether I use words or just show your love by my actions. Amen.

EVERYTHING'S GOOD

Give thanks in all circumstances;
for this is God's will for you in Christ Jesus.

1 Thessalonians 5:18

Sometimes God uses someone I don't like to teach me a lesson. Or he uses some set of circumstances I don't really enjoy to work out his will in me.

He does this to cure me of always needing to figure things out on my own or to have my own way. He wants me to learn to willingly choose his way, whether I feel like it or not.

———

God, I have to do lots of things whether I want to or not. I have to go to school, whether I feel like it or not. Sometimes I have to take medicine I don't want to take. I even have to go to church sometimes when I would rather do something else. God, keep me true to you, whether I feel like it or not. Amen.

OCTOBER

GOD IS CLOSER

"Freely you have received; freely give."

Matthew 10:8

At times, I will feel very close to God and have a strong sense of his presence.

God gives me those times to fill me with more of the Holy Spirit. Then, even when I don't feel so close to him, God still helps me bless others with what I have received from him in an earlier time.

— — — —

God, at times, I do feel very close to you; other times I wonder why I don't feel anything at all. I guess one thing I'm learning is that how I feel doesn't determine whether you're with me or not. Teach me how to be aware of your presence at all times, even when I don't feel very close to you. Amen.

I'M WALKING BY FAITH

I will follow your rules forever,
because they make me happy.

Psalm 119:111 NCV

I want to learn to walk by faith, not by feelings. The test of my faith in Jesus is whether I will be my best for him even if I don't feel like it or when nobody else is looking.

Do I live as Jesus wants me to live during those times when I don't necessarily feel his presence?

————

God, whether I feel close to you or not, let my life be of use to you and others. I know you are always with me. You're never NOT with me. Turn my heart so completely to you that you can use me to bless others, whether I feel like you're with me or not. Amen.

I KNOW GOD
AND HE KNOWS ME

I consider everything a loss because of the surpassing
worth of knowing Christ Jesus my Lord, for whose
sake I have lost all things. I consider them garbage,
that I may gain Christ and be found in him . . .

Philippians 3:8–9

T he secret of living by faith is knowing God. I can
be eager to serve God and do something for him,
but am I eager to know God?

Is it possible to be so busy doing things for God that
I don't take time to know him?

Knowing God is what makes me ready to serve God.

———

Long ago, rich people had big houses and lots of
servants. The servants could serve in the same
household for years and not really know the people
they served. Back then, servants didn't have much of
a choice, but I do. I can choose to follow you or choose
to ignore you, God. God, I don't want to just serve you,
I want to know you. Let me know your heart, O God.
Teach me what it means to know you, really know you.
Amen.

GOD KNOWS ME
INSIDE & OUT

Yet you know me, LORD;
you see me and test my thoughts about you.

Jeremiah 12:3

No one knows me better than God. He knows what I am able to do. He knows what his purpose for me is, and he knows my heart. The more I get to know God, the more clearly I will understand how he thinks about me.

I'll be ready for the exciting plans that await me as I seek to follow his will.

— — — — —

O God, teach me what it means to know you, *really* know you. Let the words that come out of my mouth and the thoughts that stay in my head be pleasing to you. And when they're not, show me how to be honest and loving at the same time. Amen.

I CHOOSE LIFE

Since we have been made right with God
by our faith, we have peace with God.
This happened through our Lord Jesus Christ.

Romans 5:1 NRSV

The Bible says all have sinned and that the penalty for sin is death. Death is separation from God. I must make a choice: life or death.

I must choose between enjoying the presence of God or being separated from him. If I refuse to follow Jesus and let him save me from my sins, I am choosing to be separated from God.

- - - - -

God, sometimes I feel pretty good about myself and sometimes, not so good. Either way—whether my sins are little or big—I know I need you. Help me accept the truth about myself and see how very much I need your grace and strength. I never want to be separated from you! Amen.

JESUS HELPS ME LIVE

Now to him who is able to do immeasurably
more than all we ask or imagine, according
to his power that is at work within us, to him
be glory in the church and in Christ Jesus
throughout all generations, for ever and ever! Amen.

Ephesians 3:20–21

I might get discouraged when I look at the teachings
of Jesus if I imagine trying to live up to them in my
own power.

The secret of God's "Good News" is that when I place
my trust in Jesus, he puts a new power in me. That is *his*
power, the Holy Spirit.

The only way I can really be a true follower of Jesus is
to live by the Holy Spirit's power.

———

God, teach me how to live by the power of the Holy
Spirit. I know your Spirit lives inside me. Show me how
to listen to his voice and be led by the Holy Spirit in
everything I do and say. Amen.

TURNING FROM WRONG TO RIGHT

We always pray for you, asking our God
to help you live the kind of life he called you to live.
We pray that with his power God will help you do
the good things you want and perform the works
that come from your faith.

2 Thessalonians 1:11 NRSV

Sin is not just doing the wrong thing; it means having the wrong idea about my relationship with God. In a way, it means I'm not allowing God to be God in my life.

When I do what I want to do, instead of what God wants me to do (sin), that's the same as wanting to be my own god. When that happens, I need to repent.

Repentance is a big word. It means praying, "I am sorry for wanting to be my own god. I am going the wrong way, my way. I will turn around and go your way."

Then God puts in me the power to do both the right thing and be right in his eyes.

— — — — —

God, forgive me for wanting to be my own god. I want you to be my God. I want to go your way, not mine. Help me to obey from the heart, so I can be right on the inside as well as the outside. Amen.

PRAYER STARTS EACH DAY

My Presence will go with you,
and I will give you rest.

Exodus 33:14

I will get into the habit of praying each morning. I will open myself to God's presence at the very start of each day. This will help me stay aware of his presence throughout the day.

I never know when or how he is going to respond to my prayers, so I want to be paying attention at all times. When he answers my prayers, I want to be sure to say, "Thank you."

— — — —

Holy Spirit, show me if there is anything in me that is preventing God from getting through to me today. Keep my eyes wide open, my heart attentive, and my ears actively listening for whatever you might be trying to say to me. Amen.

GOD FORGIVES

In Christ we are set free by the blood of his death,
and so we have forgiveness of sins.
How rich is God's grace.

Ephesians 1:7 NRSV

I will build my faith on what God has said and done,
not on my feelings.

The death of Jesus on the cross is a real event in
human history. It actually happened! At that moment in
history, Jesus paid the penalty for sin so that I could be
forgiven and clean.

I don't have to *feel* forgiven. I *am* forgiven. God says so,
and I believe it.

God, I don't have to feel forgiven. I am forgiven! I
Am Forgiven! I AM FORGIVEN! For anything and for
everything! I am a child of God, forgiven, blessed, and
precious in the sight of the One who created heaven and
the earth. That's incredible! Help me understand what
it really means that I am forgiven and that I am loved.
Amen.

I LEARN BY OBEYING

A person who does not have the Spirit
does not accept the truths that come from
the Spirit of God. That person thinks they are
foolish and cannot understand them, because they
can only be judged to be true by the Spirit.

1 Corinthians 2:14 NRSV

God can't tell me the secrets in his Word until I am willing to obey.

I will not always understand God's Word with my mind. Yet I will see what it means as I obey what it says.

God reveals more of his will to me when I obey what I already know to do. Obedience always comes before understanding.

O God, give me the strength to obey your Word in whatever limited way I now understand. And then as I obey what I know to do, show me more so I can be my best for you. Amen.

GOD HEARS MY PRAYERS

Jesus looked up and said,
"Father, I thank you that you heard me.
I knew that you always hear me . . ."

John 11:41–42 NRSV

Prayer sometimes seems useless. It can feel like no one is there to talk to.

When prayer feels like God isn't listening, I will pray even more. I will keep praying. I always can say this with confidence, "I know God has heard me."

— — — —

God, I know you hear me even when I feel so far away from you, even when I feel my prayers are useless. I pray for faith, even when doubts feel more real than your presence. Amen.

IS ANYONE LOOKING?

Nothing in all creation is hidden from God's sight.
Everything is uncovered and laid bare before the eyes
of him to whom we must give account.

Hebrews 4:13

How do I behave when no one else is looking? Do I act the same when no one else sees me as I do when I am with others?

Does it matter more to me what others think or what God thinks? He is always around and always watching and waiting for me to reach out to him.

God, sometimes I only do the right thing because I'm afraid of getting caught if I do the wrong thing. That's not what being holy is, is it? God, make me holy from the inside out so that I do the right thing just because I want to please you. Amen.

GOD'S WORK, GOD'S WAY

My message and my preaching were not with wise
and persuasive words, but with a demonstration of
the Spirit's power, so that your faith might not rest on
human wisdom, but on God's power.

1 Corinthians 2:4–5

God wants me to rely on the power of his Spirit to do his work.

He'll often allow me to go through trials until I lose confidence in my own natural abilities. Then he can teach me to trust him.

I cannot do God's work in my own human strength. I will need to learn what it means to trust his Spirit in me.

God, relying on you and not my own abilities seems hard to understand—and upside down. As a follower of Jesus, being my best means using my talents and abilities to honor you. In school, it seems like we want to do our best so others will see how great we are—and to honor ourselves. God, help me understand the relationship between being my best for you and doing my best in school, sports, and other activities. Amen.

I AM A DISCIPLE

To him who is able to keep you from stumbling and to present you before his glorious presence without fault and with great joy—to the only God our Savior be glory, majesty, power and authority, through Jesus Christ our Lord, before all ages, now and forevermore! Amen.

Jude 1:24–25

Jesus helps me do God's work by the power of the Holy Spirit inside me. The Holy Spirit keeps me from stumbling along in my own strength and instead enables me to bring glory to God.

God is the God above all gods. His Son, Jesus, must be absolute Lord of my life. I can only be his true follower by learning to do what he says and by relying on the power of the Holy Spirit.

If I try to follow Jesus' ways or do his work in my own strength, I will become discouraged. His Spirit in me gives me the power and the authority to do his work.

Jesus, be Lord of my life today. By your grace and power, help me be my best for you. Teach me what it means to live by the power of your Spirit within me and not by my own strength. Amen.

I AM A MISSIONARY

"The Spirit of the Lord is on me,
because he has anointed me to proclaim
good news to the poor."

Luke 4:18

All disciples of Jesus are called to be missionaries, to tell others the good news of Jesus. The good news is that God so loved the *world* that he gave his one and only Son.

The world! No one is left out. There isn't anyone who cannot benefit from the good news about Jesus. It is good news for everybody in the world. Now, that's something I can be excited about! I want to be a part of that picture!

— — — —

God, I want to tell others the good gews about your love. Help me to know the right person and the right time to share the truth about you. I want everyone to know how much you love us. Thanks, God. Amen.

I LOVE
THE GOOD NEWS

"Open your eyes and look at the fields!
They are ripe for harvest."

John 4:35

Jesus said I am to pray for workers to be sent out to tell the good news.

I know how easy it is to get busy with so many activities. In fact, I can get so busy I forget that people all around me need to hear the good news of Jesus' love.

Am I praying for others? Am I doing what I can to spread this good news? Or am I spending my time on too many other, less important things?

God, I've got to admit, most of my prayers are all about me. I ask for your help, tell you things I want, or pray for only those I love. I guess I can be pretty self-centered. Forgive me, God, when I forget how big the world is and how many people need to know about your love. Open my eyes to what I can do for you and others. Amen.

PRAY THEN TELL

"I tell you the truth,
whoever believes in me will do the same things
that I do. Those who believe will do even greater
things than these, because I am going to the Father."

John 14:12 NCV

Prayer that completely believes in God's power is powerful. Prayer is where battles are won. It is how I call on God to bring all his power against the power of my enemy, Satan.

I cannot defeat the devil on my own strength, but he is no match for God. In everything, I will pray first, then go and spread the good news. God will go before me and fight for me.

God, I hear things about Satan or evil that are scary and make me feel afraid. But I know nothing is more powerful than your love. I know the world has evil people, and I know evil things happen. Teach me how to pray my way through any fear, so I can be courageous for you. Let me be bold in living my life for you. Amen.

BECAUSE I LOVE

Christ's love compels us, because we are
convinced that one died for all, and therefore all died.
And he died for all, that those who live should
no longer live for themselves but for him who died
for them and was raised again.

2 Corinthians 5:14–15

The proof of my love for Jesus is found in my willingness to serve others. When I serve others with kind deeds and encouraging words, I am letting them in on the good news.

The people God uses to spread the good news of the gospel are just everyday people like me who have a deep love for Jesus and love others with his kind of love.

When I love Jesus, I will want others to know him.

Jesus, help me know when and how to tell the story of your love. Help me know when to open my mouth and when to keep it shut. Let my actions honor you, show me how to think, and let my heart be filled with you. Let all I do tell the story of your love. Amen.

SPREADING THE GOOD NEWS

"I have raised you up for this very purpose,
that I might show you my power and that my name
might be proclaimed in all the earth."

Exodus 9:16

The power I have in telling others about God depends on my personal relationship with him. If God and I are as close as best friends, others will want to know my friend too.

When I am filled with God's Spirit, all of my activity for him will be effective. I want to serve others in such a way that they will experience the presence of God.

If I don't have it, I can't give it.

Dear God, fill me with your Spirit today. However you make that happen and wherever that leads, I ask you to fill my heart, my mind, and my soul with your love. Amen.

YOUR LOVE IS AMAZING!

God demonstrates his own love for us in this:
While we were still sinners, Christ died for us.

Romans 5:8

The most amazing fact of all time is that God loved me before I knew anything about him.

Jesus' love was so great that he died on a cross, even for the very people who hated him. They were spitting on him, beating him, crowning him with thorns, and crucifying him. And still he said, "Father, forgive them."

That is amazing love!

———

God, it's no wonder the Bible says nothing can separate us from the love of God, which is in Jesus. Thank you for loving me even before I knew you. Amen.

WHO'S IN CONTROL?

Everyone who competes in the games goes
into strict training. They do it to get a crown
that will not last, but we do it to get
a crown that will last forever.

1 Corinthians 9:25

To be a disciple of Jesus means discipline and training. A small child is impulsive and does whatever feels good at the time. But a disciple of Jesus learns to grow up by bringing his or her thoughts and actions under the control of the Holy Spirit.

Do I have thoughts or reactions that have still not come under the Holy Spirit's control? I will be honest with God about these areas in my life. He will help me bring them under control.

Jesus, I want to become more like you, and I give you my heart. Along with it comes my stubbornness, my impatience, my temper, and my grouchiness. Teach me how to bring all of me under the control of your Holy Spirit. Help me learn to be a "disciple" who lives a "disciplined life." Amen.

ALIVE IN YOUR SPIRIT

Who knows a person's thoughts except their own spirit
within them? In the same way no one knows
the thoughts of God except the Spirit of God.

1 Corinthians 2:11

The way I know God is mainly through my spirit, not
my mind.

My spirit is that inner part of me that can't be seen.
God is spirit. He can only be known by my spirit. When
the Spirit of God came into my spirit, he made me alive to
him so I can know him. I want to be alive spiritually (in my
spirit). That's real living!

— — — — —

God, I know I can't see you or see my spirit. Knowing
you would be so much easier if you were visible,
huggable, and right here in front of me. Help me learn
to know you in my spirit, that deepest part of my being.
Teach me the ways of the spirit, so I can really know
you. Amen.

INSIDE OUT

You may become blameless and pure, "children of God
without fault in a warped and crooked generation."
Then you will shine among them like stars in the sky . . .

Philippians 2:15

I can't just make up my mind to change the way I behave.
I can try, but the change won't last very long.

My inner desires need to change, and then my actions
will follow. In other words, I must change from the inside
out. When God's Spirit makes me alive spiritually, he begins
to change me on the inside. I become a new creation.

Everything Jesus wants me to become is a possibility
because it is his power changing me.

— — — —

Dear God, fill me with the Holy Spirit today. However
you make that happen and wherever that leads, I ask
you to fill my heart, my mind, and my soul with your
Spirit and a desire to serve you. Change me from the
inside out. Amen.

LIFE IN THE SPIRIT

May our Lord Jesus Christ himself and God our
Father, who loved us and by his grace gave us eternal
encouragement and good hope, encourage your hearts
and strengthen you in every good deed and word.

2 Thessalonians 2:16–17

God's Spirit in me has the power to help me live according to the highest standard. That's the standard Jesus set. That's what "being my best for God" means!

I cannot do it in my own strength. But I never need to be discouraged if I fall short from time to time. I can simply get up and start again. Then the Holy Spirit's power can fill me again and give me a new start.

— — — —

Dear God, the way for me to be my best for you is to be filled with your Spirit. Fill my heart with so much of you that there's no room for anything else. Let my actions honor you, my thoughts be transformed by you, and my heart be filled with your love. Let all I do please you. Amen.

GOD, REMAKE ME

"Submit to God and be at peace with him;
in this way prosperity will come to you."

Job 22:21

I f I am going to be an effective worker for God, I must let him help me stop doing things my way.

He must teach me how to trust the working of the Holy Spirit within me.

I want God to have his way with me. I want to do God's will, not mine. I want to succeed according to his terms, not those of the world around me.

— — — —

God, sometimes it's really hard to submit to my parents and do what they want me to do. There's just something inside of me that doesn't want to be told what to do. Show me how to submit to you, to understand your ways, and to follow your will for my life. And, while you're at it, please help me to learn to be more obedient to my parents. Thank you, God. Amen.

GOD CALLING

Jesus said, "Peace be with you!
As the Father has sent me, I am sending you."

John 20:21

The needs in the world are so great. The only real solution is for people to come to know God through Jesus Christ.

Every follower of Jesus is sent out into the world to be a light. Jesus said I should go and teach all nations.

A person just like me could make a big difference. I can be bold and learn to trust God's wisdom and power. He can use me to change the world!

————

God, I want to be willing to go wherever you call me, to do whatever you ask of me. I know I can make a difference in the world. Teach me to be bold and courageous in the way I follow you. Give me enough faith to follow you no matter what it means or how much it costs. Amen.

POWER TO CHANGE

The things you have heard me say in the presence
of many witnesses entrust to reliable people who
will also be qualified to teach others.

2 Timothy 2:2

T he main mission of every disciple of Jesus is getting
more people to follow Jesus (make disciples).

When I go to make disciples, I need to always
remember what Jesus said: "all power is given to me." The
power to make disciples comes from God, not me.

I simply have to go, and he will supply the power to do
the work.

- - - - -

God, I'm not sure I understand where the line between
what I need to do and what I need to let you do through
me starts and stops. God, I want you to use me in
whatever way you can to help other people become your
followers. Help me understand what being a disciple
really means. Amen.

IT IS FINISHED

When he had received the drink, Jesus said,
"It is finished." With that, he bowed his head
and gave up his spirit.

John 19:30

I t is hard to understand what Jesus did on the cross.
My mind can't fully grasp it.

I simply will believe the Bible and be grateful that
he loved me enough to die in my place. The Bible says
because of his death on the cross, I can be put into a right
relationship with God.

"It is finished" means everything that needs to be done
to make me a new creation has already been done.

It's finished.

God, I've got to admit, some things in the Bible are
really hard to understand with my mind. So if logic and
brain power aren't the main requirements in knowing
you, give me the kind of understanding I need to
appreciate all you've done to make me your child. Amen.

JESUS MAKES ME CLEAN

God made him who had no sin to be sin for us,
so that in him we might become
the righteousness of God.

2 Corinthians 5:21

My sins are removed because of the death of Jesus on the cross. I am acceptable to God because I have been forgiven and made clean. Jesus took my sin on himself so that nothing need ever come between me and God.

— — — —

God, in the death and resurrection of Jesus, you made it possible for me to call you Father. You took on human form and made a way for me to come into your holy presence. That's incredible! The God who made the heavens and the earth calls me by name and wants to have fellowship with me. God, I pray for the boldness to accept this incredible truth—and the boldness to believe that I can call you my heavenly Father. Amen.

BELIEVING
WHAT I CAN'T SEE

Without faith it is impossible to please God,
because anyone who comes to him must believe
that he exists and that he rewards those
who earnestly seek him.

Hebrews 11:6

The disciple of Jesus lives by faith.
Faith is not the same as common sense. Faith is
believing things I cannot see or figure out with my mind.
It is believing in God and his Word even when it doesn't
make sense to my natural way of thinking. It is believing
God and acting on that belief no matter what.

———————

Believing and seeing are not the same thing. I know
some things with my mind, but some things can only
be known with my heart. God, help me believe beyond
what my mind sees. Can I see the air I breathe? No, but
I know it's there, or I wouldn't be alive. Can I see my
heart beating? No, but I can feel my heart beat. Can
I see the person at the other end of the telephone?
No, but I know the person is there. I believe things I
can't see every day. Just because I can't see something
doesn't mean it's not real. And just because I can't see
you, God, doesn't mean you aren't there. Amen.

319

FAITH FIGHTS

Fight the good fight of the faith.
Take hold of the eternal life to which you
were called when you made your good confession
in the presence of many witnesses.

1 Timothy 6:12

Faith is a fight.
I must constantly be on guard against anything that
would weaken or destroy my faith. My faith must be rooted
in the character of God. Circumstances change, but God
does not. Even though my faith will be tested, I can always
trust in God. And faith in God is worth fighting for.

— — — —

God, today I rest in you. I give you all my questions,
desires, dreams, and fears. I know some days will be
wonderful, and some days will be lousy. Today, I accept
today as a gift, no matter what comes my way. Make
my faith strong enough to ride the ups and downs that
come with being human. Make mine a "fighting faith."
Amen.

NOVEMBER

I BELONG TO GOD

Jesus answered,
"Will you really lay down your life for me?"
John 13:38

The truth is I do not belong to myself. I belong to God. The more real that idea becomes to me, the more I will want God to use me to serve others. No more "me first!"

Two things matter more than almost everything else: first, I want God to have his way in me; second, I want the way I live to make others hungry for a taste of his love.

Do I have any other plans for my life?

― ― ― ―

God, I have a lot of hopes and dreams, but I'm not really sure what my plans are or if I even have any. I don't usually think that far ahead. So, God, when I do make plans, let my plans be your plans. Let me honor you with every step I take and serve you in all that I do. Amen.

A LIFE OF LOVE

"If you love me, keep my commands."

John 14:15

J esus didn't come to give me a new set of rules to live by. Jesus modeled a way of life for me to imitate. If my relationship with him is based on love, I will want to live according to his model. And I will do it willingly, wholeheartedly, and without argument. I will obey him because my spirit—the real me—will agree with the Holy Spirit who lives in me that Jesus is Lord.

Jesus, make my understanding of serving you bigger than rules or right and wrong. Fill me with a longing to love you, the grace to grow in you, and the desire to serve you. Amen.

THE CROSS IN MY LIFE

I have been crucified with Christ and I no
longer live, but Christ lives in me. The life I now
live in the body, I live by faith in the Son of God,
who loved me and gave himself for me.

Galatians 2:20

"I am crucified with Christ" means I have the same
attitude that Jesus had when he went to the cross.
He gave up all of his natural rights. Even though he was
God, he died like a helpless man because he knew it was
God's will for him.

God doesn't just want me to give up things. He wants me
to be so alive to him that I have little interest in anything but
doing his will. That's what "I no longer live" means.

- - - -

God, give me the ability to grow in understanding the
ways in which you work in my life. I ask you for patience
with what doesn't make sense, trust in all that I don't
understand, and rest in everything that I question.
Amen.

DOING WHAT I KNOW TO DO

Do not merely listen to the word and so deceive
yourselves. Do what it says.

James 1:22

I will only really understand a truth of God when I am
willing to act on it. Just reading the words of Jesus in the
Bible and saying, "My, that is a nice truth!" isn't enough.

I will only be fully alive in God in those times when I
completely obey what I see in God's Word. When my heart
is willing to obey, I will understand what God wants me to
do and be.

— — — —

God, I want to be fully alive in you. I want to have the
courage to put my faith into action. I want to make a
difference for you in the world around me. Increase my
understanding and create in me a passionate desire to
obey your Word. Amen.

NO SHORTCUTS

Be glad that you are sharing Christ's sufferings,
so that you may be full of joy when his glory is revealed.

1 Peter 4:13

Nobody likes to suffer. Wanting a shortcut to becoming a true disciple of Jesus is a natural thing. But even Jesus suffered and "learned obedience" through his suffering. As his disciple, I must be willing to go through trials also.

When I am in agreement with God's purposes, I will understand how he is dealing with me. As a follower of Jesus, I will often understand God's ways only after I obey.

— — — —

God, I think understanding must be one of those things like wisdom: it only comes with time and gray hair. But until I'm old enough to have gray hair and the wisdom that comes with it, I just ask you for a heart willing to obey your Word and follow your ways. Amen.

WHAT IT MEANS TO BELIEVE

"I am the resurrection and the life.
The one who believes in me will live,
even though they die; and whoever lives
by believing in me will never die."

John 11:25–26

Belief is not giving a mental yes to Jesus. It means I act on that belief; in other words, it means I obey. To believe not only means I have faith *in* him, but it also means I commit to being faithful *to* him.

Once I really believe from the heart (obey), I will be amazed I didn't do it sooner.

- - - -

One of the stories in the Bible is about a man who came to Jesus and asked him to heal his son. "Jesus said, 'All things can be done for the one who believes,'; the father immediately said, 'Lord, I believe; help my unbelief'" (Mark 9:23–24). When it comes to belief, those words are a prayer for any follower of Jesus. Jesus, I believe but help my unbelief. Help me in all the ways I struggle to believe. Amen.

IT'S UNDER CONTROL

The fruit of that righteousness will be peace;
its effect will be quietness and confidence forever.

Isaiah 32:17

Nothing takes God by surprise.

God will sometimes allow me to experience things I cannot understand at all. That's when he wants me to learn to trust him. I should trust that all of my life is in his hands.

If I am in the middle of something I don't understand right now, God's message to me is clear: "Relax. Quit worrying and fussing. Be quiet! Let me use this experience to teach you something very special. You can have full confidence in me."

— — — —

God, I want to draw near to you. Help me learn how to do that, especially when I don't get what's going on. And when I'm not getting it, draw me near to you. Amen.

I AM A TEMPLE

The Spirit also comes to help us, weak as we are.
For we do not know how we ought to pray;
the Spirit himself pleads with God for us in groans that
words cannot express.

Romans 8:26 GNB

My body is "a temple of the Holy Spirit." A temple is a place to pray. That is what the Holy Spirit does in me. He prays.

Because he is the Spirit of God, he knows the mind of God. Since this is true, the Holy Spirit in me always prays according to the will of God.

He is praying in me now.

———

Holy Spirit, I ask you to help me pray, even when I feel like I don't know what I'm doing. Could you fill in the gaps when I don't know what to pray? And could you help me learn what prayer is really all about? Thank you, God. Amen.

SPIRIT AND WORD

The word of God is alive and active.
Sharper than any double-edged sword, it penetrates
even to dividing soul and spirit, joints and marrow;
it judges the thoughts and attitudes of the heart.

Hebrews 4:12

Doing a good job telling others about Jesus does not depend on my personality or cleverness. Rather, it depends on the power of the Word of God and the Spirit of God. When I share things from the Word of God with others, the Spirit of God will help them want to know God and will use what I share.

The Word of God is alive and active. It's not so much that we read the Bible but that the Bible reads us. It shows us who we really are and creates in us a desire to become everything God created us to be.

God, I'm going to do what I think you are telling me to do and then leave the results to you. Do I have that right? That seems so easy, like taking a test but not worrying about the grade. Teach me how to trust you like that—to do what I think is right and leave the rest to you. Amen.

LISTENING TO GOD

"My Father, if it is possible, may this cup
be taken from me. Yet not as I will but as you will."

Matthew 26:39

When I say, "I am going to do this or that with my life,"
I need to add, "if it is your will, God." Putting any
personal plans or interests ahead of my Lord's will keep
God from getting through to me with his plans.

I want to learn to stop telling God what I want long
enough for God to tell me what he wants.

— — — —

God, put a stopper in my mouth and unplug my ears. Let
me learn to listen long enough, so I can hear you in ways
too obvious to miss. Thanks, God. Amen.

OBEY, DON'T DELAY

We take captive every thought
to make it obedient to Christ.

2 Corinthians 10:5

I want to learn to say yes to God as soon as I see some new truth in his Word. I don't want to hesitate by thinking about how it will affect my life or the lives of those around me.

I just want to obey immediately! God will always take care of relationships that are affected by my obedience to his Word.

God, a lot of adults tell me to think before I act. It seems like you say to act before I think. Which is it, God? Help me know when to leap before I look. Other times, help me to walk up to the edge of the cliff and think before taking a flying leap. I know I won't always get it right, God, but I'm willing to give it my best. Amen.

EVERYTHING NEW
IN YOU

We were therefore buried with him through
baptism into death in order that, just as Christ
was raised from the dead through the glory
of the Father, we too may live a new life.

Romans 6:4

T he Holy Spirit makes me a new creation.
I am really changed. I no longer think the same
way about God, others, or myself.

My desires are becoming new. Things that used to
control me are losing their power. The Holy Spirit is the
new source of life in me. He can make everything new.

- - - - -

Jesus, keep my faith in you new and never let me take
knowing you for granted. Thank you for giving me life,
this day, this moment, and all that is yet to be. Amen.

WORSHIP STARTS IN THE HEART

"Worthy is the Lamb, who was slain,
to receive power and wealth and wisdom
and strength and honor and glory and praise!"

Revelation 5:12

Spiritual growth comes as I spend time worshiping God with all my heart. Learning to worship God with my whole heart means coming into God's presence with my heart full of thanksgiving and praise.

It means thanking him for saving me from myself and my sin and giving me the Holy Spirit. And I thank him for bringing me into his pure and holy presence as his child.

God is worthy of all my praise!

———

God, draw me into your presence in these few moments of quietness. Thank you for the gift of life that comes from knowing Jesus as my Lord and Savior. Fill me with the Holy Spirit and deepen my understanding of what it means to live as a child of God. Help me to know I am loved by the Lord God Almighty, today and every day. Amen.

HE'S BY MY SIDE

If we live by the Spirit,
let us also be guided by the Spirit.

Galatians 5:25 NRSV

I can be in such close communication with God that I do not have to continually ask him to guide me.

When I am walking in step with his Spirit, my common-sense decisions are most often his will for me. And if I am going the wrong direction, he will check me and bring me back into agreement with his purposes.

– – – – –

Jesus, keep me in step with the Holy Spirit. Let your Word be my guide. Let your Spirit shape my thoughts. And let me be my best for you. Amen.

KEEPING JESUS
IN VIEW

We continually ask God to fill you with
the knowledge of his will through all the wisdom
and understanding that the Spirit gives.

Colossians 1:9

With God's help, I will stay focused on Jesus. I won't be distracted from my loyalty to Jesus by getting involved in things that don't concern me.

In any situation that comes up, I will pray and ask God what I am to do and what I am not to do. Then I will do what he says. That is wisdom.

God, I can be just as distracted by good things in someone else's life as I can be by the bad. Instead of thinking about what's fair or what's not fair, keep me focused on you. I want to learn to trust you. I want to learn I can trust you not only with my life but with the lives of all those I love as well. Amen.

BEING GREAT
OR BEING FAMOUS

Do nothing out of selfish ambition or vain conceit.
Rather, in humility value others above yourselves.

Philippians 2:3

I don't need to look for something great to do for God. The greatest thing a disciple of Jesus does is to faithfully and quietly serve him in the everyday, ordinary things. I really don't need attention or recognition from anyone.

Being humble means accepting my place in God's kingdom, whether great or small, with joy. If I do something great someday, I would want people to say, "What a great God you serve!" That would mean more to me than hearing them say, "What a wonderful person you are."

God, here I am. I give all of me, good and bad, to your care and keeping. Let everything I do be to honor you. Thank you for the gift of life today. Amen.

GOD IS THE BEST

"You are worthy, our Lord and God, to receive glory
and honor and power, for you created all things, and by
your will they were created and have their being."

Revelation 4:11

I want to make God my goal. I want to get to know him at any cost. There is no price too high to pay for knowing my Creator-Father. I always want to be willing to say no to anything that could keep me from saying yes to him.

The almighty God of heaven—my Creator and Father—is waiting to reveal himself to me. I don't want to miss out on anything he has for me.

God, teach me how to say no to anything that would keep me from saying yes to you. Whatever it costs, whatever it takes, and whatever it means, I want to know you and be my best for you! Amen.

HOW TO BE FREE

"If the Son sets you free,
you will be free indeed."

John 8:36

God will set me free from some things. There are other areas of my life in which I will be set free by making right choices.

The cross of Jesus has made it possible for me to be free from the power of sin, but I must choose daily to go God's way instead of my own.

The Holy Spirit will give me power as I cooperate with him. The more godly choices I make, the more natural it will become for me to make more godly choices. Godly choices eventually become godly habits.

God, help me to cooperate for a change!

God, here's how it seems to work: I make choices, but you give me the power to change. As I cooperate with you, the Holy Spirit comes alongside me and gives me the power to change the things that are not pleasing to you. So what I need to do is to learn to cooperate with the Holy Spirit for a change. God, teach me how to do that. Amen.

THE MIRACLE
OF FORGIVENESS

Against you, you only,
have I sinned and done what is evil in your sight.

Psalm 51:4

Forgiveness is the great miracle of the love of God.
I don't deserve it, but God forgives me because of Jesus.
I will only be truly sorry for my sin when I see that I have
turned my back on the love and grace of God by sinning. All
sin is a sin against the love of God.

Refusing to confess is refusing to accept the love and
forgiveness of God. If there's anything in my life that's
not pleasing to God, I won't wait any longer. I will ask his
forgiveness right now.

— — — —

Being forgiven is like taking a bath but getting clean on
the inside. Everyone does stuff they wish they hadn't.
That's part of being human. But when we've hurt a
friend, been dishonest with our parents, gotten really
mad at a brother or sister, or said something we wish we
hadn't, by confessing we let God make us clean from the
inside out.

FORGIVENESS MEANS LOVE

In him we have . . .
the forgiveness of sins.

Ephesians 1:7

F orgiveness is the most powerful proof of God's love, and the cross of Jesus is the most incredible reminder of the love of God.

The God of love offered us forgiveness while we were still his enemies. How can I ever question the love of my heavenly Father?

God, I want to be my best for you since you gave your best for me. You gave your only Son. Forgive me when I fail to please you. Let me live today in the fullness of your love, trusting that your love is always greater than my sin. Amen.

THE COST OF FORGIVENESS

Let those who love the Lord hate evil,
for he guards the lives of his faithful ones
and delivers them from the hand of the wicked.

Psalm 97:10

The cross on which Jesus suffered is the clearest picture of how much God hates sin. God hates sin that much! How can I continue to hold onto sin when it cost God such a great price?

Asking God to help me hate sin as much as he does is the path to being my best for him.

———

O God, I am so sorry for what my sin cost you. I confess it and forsake it. Give me a holy hatred for sin. Have mercy on me for the sake of your Son, Jesus. Amen.

ENJOYING GOD

Whether you eat or drink or whatever you do, do it all
for the glory of God.

1 Corinthians 10:31

I don't need to take myself too seriously. I need to learn
to enjoy God in the ordinary details of life: eating,
drinking, laughing, playing, and everything!

I can even learn to laugh at myself when I make a mistake.

Being a follower of Jesus is the best life ever. A follower
of Jesus can have more fun than anyone! Being a disciple
of Jesus doesn't mean being so heavenly-minded that I'm
no earthly good.

God, keep my eyes wide open to your presence in my
life, and if I fall asleep spiritually, wake me up. Help me
to picture doing life with you by my side and enjoying
everything we do together. Remind me you're there
when I take myself too seriously and start to get cranky.
I love being your child, and I love that you enjoy being
my Father. Amen.

DISTRACTIONS

Leave all your worries with him,
because he cares for you.

1 Peter 5:7 GNB

S imple things have incredible power to distract me from God. Jesus said he cares of this world can choke out what he wants to do in me.

Do I have cares and concerns I haven't been able to hand over to my Father in heaven? Are they distracting me from focusing on my walk with him?

— — — —

God, I give you my life today. I give you my future. And I want to give you all the worry that comes in between. Keep me from being distracted by all the things around me, and teach me to focus my eyes on you. Amen.

I'M STAYING FOCUSED

My eyes are fixed on you,
Sovereign LORD; in you I take refuge.

Psalm 141:8

Are my eyes and ears focused on God? Am I looking to him to lead and guide me? If not, I run the risk of being influenced by all the wrong opinions and listening only to human reason.

Human reason and worldly opinions will seldom agree with God's purposes for me. I need to keep focused on him, so I can become what he wants me to be.

— — — — —

God, like sunlight coming into my window in the morning, bring the light of your loving presence into my world. Keep me centered on you. Help me see myself honestly, and please bring your light to any dark emotions like anger, resentment, or jealousy that try to take hold of my heart today. Amen.

THE CROSS
MEANS FORGIVEN

May I never boast except in the cross of our
Lord Jesus Christ, through which the world
has been crucified to me, and I to the world.

Galatians 6:14

The cross of Christ is the power of God. When I come
to the cross of Jesus for forgiveness, I come into touch
with the power of God.

When I tell others about what Jesus did on the cross,
the power of God is at work in those who listen. Then
they can respond to the powerful love of God. That is why
the apostle Paul said, "We preach Christ crucified . . . the
power of God" (1 Corinthians 1:23–24).

God, let my actions honor you. Let my thoughts be
transformed by you. Let my heart be filled with you. By
the power of the cross of Christ, let all I do please you.
Amen.

THE CROSS, GOD'S POWER

Christ did not send me to baptize.
He sent me to tell the Good News,
and to tell it without using the language
of human wisdom, in order to make sure that
Christ's death on the cross is not robbed of its power.

1 Corinthians 1:17 GNB

When I "go and make disciples" I tell others about what Jesus did to save me from my sin. The most important truth I can present is "the cross of our Lord Jesus Christ." The cross is not only the center of human history, but it is the focus of the power of God.

The message about the cross is what breaks us loose from the power of our sin and selfishness and sets us free to say yes to God.

- - - -

Jesus, help me know when and how to tell the story of your love. Help me know when to open my mouth and when to keep it shut. Let my life tell the story of your love, and when words are necessary, show me what to say. Amen.

THE CROSS
AND THE WORLD

Do not love the world or anything in the world.
If anyone loves the world,
love for the Father is not in them.

1 John 2:15

Jesus lived in this world, yet he never allowed this world to detract him from his mission. Like Jesus, I must live in this world, yet I can resist the temptation to let the things of this world distract me from my purpose.

Jesus taught that I live "in" the world but I am not "of" the world. I can live in this world, but I am a citizen of another world, the kingdom of God.

I never want the "spirit of this world" to get into me. It will drive out the Holy Spirit.

- - - - -

Dear God, fill me with the Holy Spirit today. Leave no room for anything else, especially the spirit of this world. However you make that happen and wherever that leads, I ask you to fill my heart, my mind, and my soul with your love and with a single-minded devotion to you. Amen.

FREE MEANS FREE

For it is by grace you have been saved, through faith—
and this is not from yourselves, it is the gift of God—
not by works, so that no one can boast.

Ephesians 2:8–9

God is an "everything I have is yours" kind of God. All is free. That is what grace means.

I have nothing to offer anyway. I come to him empty, ready, and only to receive. But God can do nothing for me until I come to him with nothing. He is everything. And he has everything I need.

———

God, I want to come to you empty of self and ready to receive. I don't want my life to be all about me. I want it to be about you. You created me to be a container for you. Fill my container so full that others will see how great you are and lose sight of me. Amen.

349

MORE THAN JUST AN EXAMPLE

"No one can see the kingdom of God
without being born from above."

John 3:3 NRSV

Many think of Jesus as a pattern or example to be followed. Jesus *is* that, but he is much, much more. He is the Son of God, the King of Kings, and Lord of Lords.

When I am "born again," God puts his holy life, the Holy Spirit, and his holy power into me.

If I only believe Jesus was a good teacher and example to follow, I am missing the real truth. The key to living a godly lifestyle is knowing that the true God is living in me by his Spirit.

- - - - -

Jesus, I know you are much more than just a good example, because you gave so much more than just a good example. You gave your life. Lord, fill my heart with so much gratitude that I want nothing more than to give my life back to you. Let me know the joy of loving you. Amen.

THE IMPOSSIBLE
IS POSSIBLE

By the grace of God I am what I am,
and his grace to me was not without effect.
No, I worked harder than all of them—yet not I,
but the grace of God that was with me.

1 Corinthians 15:10

To say it is impossible to obey the teachings of Jesus is to say he died on the cross and sent the Holy Spirit for nothing. Either I believe the Holy Spirit can make me like Jesus, or I don't believe what the Word of God says.

Am I actually becoming more like Jesus? Or am I just saying I believe certain things but not practicing what I say I believe?

— — — —

Lord, help me to put actions to my beliefs. Teach me how to be true to what I believe by lining my behavior up with my beliefs. I believe you have put your Spirit inside me to help me become more like Jesus. Now, help me learn how to cooperate with the Holy Spirit to make that happen in my everyday life. Amen.

DECEMBER

THE LAW IS A LIGHT

Whoever keeps the whole law
and yet stumbles at just one point is
guilty of breaking all of it.

James 2:10

The purpose of God's law is to show me that I can't keep the law—that I need help. Until I see that I am a sinner in need of God's help, I won't see my need of a Savior.

As soon as I confess (admit) my sin, turn from going my own way, and choose to obey God, God immediately comes to help me love his laws and follow his ways. When I love God from my heart, I love his laws and walk in his ways.

––––––

Jesus, I'm not sure I really want to see my sin the way God sees it. But I know I don't want anything to harden my heart to your love, so show me what I need to see. Let me see anything that keeps me from being my best for you. Amen.

HELPING OTHERS
WANT GOD

Not that I have already obtained all this,
or have already arrived at my goal, but I press
on to take hold of that for which Christ Jesus
took hold of me.

Philippians 3:12

Being perfect doesn't mean I never sin. It's about having a perfect (mature) relationship with God. God is not growing our relationship, so he can show people how great I am.

He wants to get me to live so close to him that my life creates a hunger in others to have a taste of his love.

Lord Jesus, help me love you with all my heart, soul, and mind. Create in me a deep, passionate love for you, and through that love, let others come to know you. Amen.

GOD'S KINGDOM: UNSHAKEABLE

Stand firm. Let nothing move you.
Always give yourselves fully to the work of the Lord,
because you know that your labor
in the Lord is not in vain.

1 Corinthians 15:58

Experiences come and go. They can't be trusted. My faith must be rooted in God. God is unshakable.

If I put my faith in how well my experiences work out, anything negative that happens is likely to upset my trust in God. If my faith is in God, nothing can ever shake it, because God cannot be shaken.

- - - -

God, I want to base my life on what I know will never fail. That can only mean putting my faith in you. Use every experience I have, the good ones, the bad ones, and everything in between, to deepen my faith in you. Amen.

STAYING
SPIRITUALLY HEALTHY

You were taught, with regard to your former way of life,
to put off your old self, which is being corrupted by
its deceitful desires; to be made new in the attitude
of your minds; and to put on the new self, created to be
like God in true righteousness and holiness.

Ephesians 4:22–24

My body stays healthy by fighting things that would make me sick, such as hunger, cold, disease, or infection. Spiritually the same thing happens. I stay healthy by fighting off sinful attitudes, behaviors, and bad choices that would weaken my spirit.

By saying yes to life-giving choices and doing the right thing, I build up a resistance to things that would make me spiritually sick.

— — — —

Jesus, today I choose to follow you. I may forget that I made that choice, but if I forget, grab my attention and remind me that even the littlest choices matter to you. I pray that my choices today will be guided by your love and mercy. Amen.

KEEPING
MY TEMPLE CLEAN

The Lord is faithful, and he will strengthen you
and protect you from the evil one.

2 Thessalonians 3:3

My body is the temple of the Holy Spirit. If I want the
Holy Spirit to be at home in my temple, I must keep
it clean and healthy.

I will ask the Holy Spirit to help me discover ways to
cleanse my body and mind. The more I train my mind and
body to obey God, the more normal it will become for me
to choose the will of God and turn away from sin.

God, help me meet today's challenges and give me
courage to face my fear. I also need your wisdom to
make good choices, to follow your will. And God, if you
give me all that today, then I know I can leave any fears
about tomorrow in your hands. Amen.

EVERYTHING I NEED

He has given us his very great and precious promises,
so that through them you may participate in the
divine nature, having escaped the corruption in the
world caused by evil desires.

2 Peter 1:4

I don't need to wait for God to do anything more for me.
God has done everything necessary to make me holy.
He has brought me into a perfect relationship with himself.
Through his Spirit within me, I learn how to work godly
qualities into my life: his joy, his peace, his love—everything!

Everything God is and has is available to me. I won't be
able to fully share in them unless I decide to lay aside my
own will and choose only his.

If I will give him everything I have, he will make
everything he has available to me. What an incredible offer!

— — — —

Dear God, be so at home in my heart that becoming
more like Jesus happens as naturally as taking my next
breath. Remove from me anything that stands in the
way of being my best for you. Teach me to be like Jesus
so that I can trust your promises as completely as Jesus
did. Amen.

ALL SIN
IS AGAINST GOD

"When he [the Holy Spirit] comes, he will prove
to the people of the world that they are wrong about sin
and about what is right and about God's judgment."

John 16:8 GNB

C onviction of sin is when the Holy Spirit makes me feel
uncomfortable inside about something I have said or
thought or done.

Being convicted of sin is *not* being sorry because I
made a mistake or got caught doing something wrong.
Conviction of sin is when the Holy Spirit shows me that I
have disappointed God by not being everything I can be.

I want to be able to say, "I have sinned against God,"
and I want to mean it. That is a sign that I have a healthy
personal relationship with him.

— — — — —

Holy Spirit, thank you for the way you make me feel
uncomfortable inside when I have done something, said
something, or even had a thought about something that
is not pleasing to God. Teach me to be quick to confess
my sins so that I can be forgiven and have a sense of
your presence again. Amen.

GOD'S BLESSINGS
ARE A GIFT

He has saved us and called us to a holy life—
not because of anything we have done but because
of his own purpose and grace. This grace was given us
in Christ Jesus before the beginning of time.

2 Timothy 1:9

There is only one way to begin a relationship with God. It is through accepting what Jesus did on the cross and saying, "I will follow you whatever it means." Then all the blessings of almighty God are mine.

No one can win God's favor or earn his blessings. They are gifts I receive when I confess my sins and make Jesus Lord of my life.

O God, I know I must make a choice. Show me how to let your life live in me so that sin can't. I want you to rule my life, not sin. So help me be my best for you, today, tomorrow and every day. Amen.

I HATE SIN

Then I acknowledged my sin to you and did not cover
up my iniquity. I said, "I will confess my transgressions
to the Lord." And you forgave the guilt of my sin.

Psalm 32:5

I want to learn to hate sin. I will have nothing to do with
it in any way, shape, or form.

But that is something I will only learn when the Holy
Spirit reveals to me the true meaning of the cross and how
sad my sin makes God. That is the only way I will want to
confess and turn away from my sins.

— — — —

God, right now I have a hard time even knowing what
sin is, much less hating it. How do I hate something I'm
not sure I can even recognize? God, I think the Holy
Spirit has a big job to do in my life. Whatever the Holy
Spirit needs to do in my life, give me a heart willing to
listen and learn. Amen.

A LIVING SACRIFICE

I urge you, brothers and sisters,
in view of God's mercy, to offer your bodies
as a living sacrifice, holy and pleasing to God—
this is your true and proper worship.

Romans 12:1

To be a disciple of Jesus I must be willing to submit my entire self—body, soul, and spirit—to God. I will only grow in my faith as I learn to discipline myself physically, mentally, and spiritually.

Most loving parents will discipline their children, so they don't make serious mistakes later in life. The same is true spiritually.

If I do not practice discipline in my spiritual life, I will fail to be truly useful in the work God has planned for me. Discipline now means joy later.

But, Jesus, I know there's a reason behind everything you say. Even if I don't think I can do what you've commanded, I want to be willing. Help me want to have the desire to do what you want me to do. Help me, dear God, to want to want to be my best for you. Amen.

WANTING GOD'S WAY

"This, then, is how you should pray:
'Our Father in heaven, hallowed be your name,
your kingdom come, your will be done,
on earth as it is in heaven.'"

Matthew 6:9–10

I want to be in control of my life. That is natural, but I have been created to live a life surrendered to God. That is super-natural.

What hurts my growth as a follower of Jesus more than anything else is saying, "I want my own way." If I am going to be a disciple of Jesus, I must die to (completely let go of) my own way. Besides, God has a much better way.

— — — — —

God, I want to do it your way. When I play with friends, I want my actions to please you. When I play sports, I want to do my best for you. When I'm hanging out at home, I want to be the person you created me to be. I don't want to be a crabby, grouchy, whining, or demanding kid. Show me how to live each day your way, not mine. Amen.

AGREEING WITH GOD

"I have given them the glory that you gave me,
that they may be one as we are one."

John 17:22

I f the Spirit of God has really turned my heart toward God and given me a love for him, I will no longer insist on my own way. I will pray, "Lord, I want to be one with you and your purposes for my life."

At that point, the Spirit of God will begin to set me free to be everything God created me to be. It's always best to agree with God.

— — — —

Lord, I do want to be one with you and your purposes for my life. Let my actions honor you. Let my thoughts be transformed by you. Let my heart be filled with you. Let all I do please you. Amen.

A DEEP WAY
TO PRAY

I urge, then, first of all, that petitions, prayers,
intercession and thanksgiving be made for all people.

1 Timothy 2:1

I ntercession is a deep form of prayer for another person.
When God calls me to pray for another person, he will
sometimes show me how he feels about that person.
Then I can pray with God's heart.

God's heart is full of hope and love. He knows the
power of Jesus to heal and save anyone in any situation.

God, I pray for those I love and those who suffer. I pray
for my friends and for every kid who is hungry, scared,
or sick. I pray for my dad and mom who have to make
tough decisions. And God, when I pray, give me your
heart for the people I am praying for. Amen.

OBEDIENCE BRINGS PEACE

"Peace I leave with you; my peace I give you.
I do not give to you as the world gives.
Do not let your hearts be troubled and do not be afraid."

John 14:27

Whenever I obey God, he will give me a sense of peace in my heart. I will have a sense of his pleasure with me. Whenever I don't have God's peace in my heart—maybe I feel restless or anxious—I will want to ask God why it's not there.

I will only get God's peace when I quit arguing with him about who is in charge. It's all about giving up trying to have my own way.

Dear God, I know being my best for you means letting Jesus live within my heart. Please fill my heart with so much of you that there's no room for anything else. Fill me, God, with your love and compassion. Give me the peace that comes from obeying you. Amen.

GOD'S WORD
IN MY HEART

Do your best to present yourself to God
as one approved, a worker who does not need to be
ashamed and who correctly handles the word of truth.

2 Timothy 2:15

Do I read God's Word regularly?
I wouldn't do very well in school if I didn't study.
Neither will I grow very much spiritually if I don't apply
myself to reading God's Word, the Bible.

Hiding God's Word in my heart will not only help me
grow, it will help me learn how to be my best for God.

Lord, "Your Word is a lamp to my feet and a light to my
path" (Psalm 119:105). Keep me walking in your ways
and growing in your Spirit. Amen.

WORD, SPIRIT, AND PRAYER

Put on the full armor of God, so that when the day
of evil comes, you may be able to stand your ground,
and after you have done everything, to stand.

Ephesians 6:13

Faith is a fight. The weapons I can use in this battle are the Word of God, the power of his Spirit, and prayer. I must learn how to use all three.

God is for me and will fight for me. No one can stand against me. No one can defeat me if I only learn how to fight. The weapons God supplies me with are powerful.

God, teach me how to use the weapons of faith. Put your Word in my heart. Teach me how to pray. And fill my soul with the power of your Spirit. I want to be one who runs the race and crosses the finish line. I don't want to sit on the sideline. Amen.

WAKING UP OTHERS

Come back to your senses as you ought,
and stop sinning; for there are some who
are ignorant of God—I say this to your shame.

1 Corinthians 15:34

S ome of my friends may not think they need God.
They are satisfied with the way things are.
They are "asleep in their sins."

I will pray that God would wake them up to their need
of a Savior. I'll pray they would become dissatisfied with the
way they live and turn toward God. I will pray they would
choose God's way instead of insisting on going their own way.

Thank you, God, for letting me get to know you while I'm
still young. I have a whole lifetime to enjoy your love. I
do pray for those who are blind to your presence. Open
their eyes. Touch their hearts. And draw them into your
loving embrace. I want everyone to know the comfort,
joy, and peace that comes from a life lived with you at
the center. Amen.

PRAY AND SEE

We know that in all things God works
for the good of those who love him,
who have been called according to his purpose.

Romans 8:28

F ollowers of Jesus believe that God can use any circumstance to work out his purposes.

Bad things happen to all of us at some point. Either we make a mistake, or someone else does something unkind to us, or maybe there's an accident. Many people believe that God doesn't have the power to bring good out of each and every event.

I believe God can bring something good out of even the most challenging circumstances. Therefore I can learn to be thankful even during difficult times.

— — — —

God, as I grow in my knowledge of you, help me grow in understanding and in faith. Help me to learn to understand your ways and give me the faith to believe in you even when I don't understand. Amen.

GOD'S TENDER HEART

For we do not have a high priest who is
unable to empathize with our weaknesses.

Hebrews 4:15

God is not a hard-hearted God who doesn't care about
my problems. God's heart is softer and more tender
than I can ever imagine.

Even though it makes God's heart sad, there is suffering
in this world. God is always hoping it will bring people
closer to him. And he is always the nearest when we hurt
the most.

We love it when God blesses us. However, sometimes
the biggest blessings come through the most difficult
circumstances.

— — — —

God, I know that even those who follow you will go
through difficult times. That's just a part of life. But I
know you can make something good come out of the
most difficult experiences. And I know your heart is
sad when you see your children suffering. Thank you for
your tender heart. Amen.

THE ONLY HOPE

"And I, when I am lifted up from the earth,
will draw all people to myself."

John 12:32

Jesus' death on the cross is the only hope for the whole world.

If I want to be effective in working for God I will tell others about how he died so that we could come to God. He became like us, so we could become more like him— so we could enjoy a loving relationship with God.

Every path to God leads through the cross of Jesus Christ.

— — — —

Jesus, thank you that I'm growing up in a home that understands the incredible gift of love that came into the world with your birth. Help me learn to celebrate you as much as I celebrate opening gifts, baking cookies, and being with family and friends. Help me learn what it means to share the gift of your love. Amen.

THE UNSEEN WORLD

The person with the Spirit
makes judgments about all things.

1 Corinthians 2:15

There is a world that is more real than the world I see. The spiritual world is real. The Holy Spirit can enable me to see the realities of this other world.

Only when a person surrenders to Jesus and receives the Holy Spirit, can he or she see the truth of God and the truth about this unseen world.

God, the world I see around me every day seems pretty real to me. But help me understand more about the unseen world around me. Help me understand the spiritual world. Make the world of your Spirit so real to me that Jesus truly does become my best friend. Make Jesus more real to me than anyone or anything I can see. Amen.

GOD CAN'T
CHOOSE FOR ME

"No one can come to me unless
the Father who sent me draws them,
and I will raise them up at the last day."

John 6:44

When God draws a person to Jesus, that person must make a choice: "Will I believe?"

Belief is not simply a mental act. Belief is a deliberate choice to obey God. That choice means turning away from the ways I used to believe and think and behave. The real question is, "Will I surrender my life to this God I can't see?"

Jesus, I choose to let you be Lord of my life. I choose to believe in you. Help me, O God, when I'm distracted from what's most important, which is loving you. When my belief is weak and my choices are less than my best, draw me close to you. I never want to lose sight of your will for my life. Amen.

CLOSE FRIENDS

The world and its desires pass away,
but whoever does the will of God lives forever.

1 John 2:17

Do I want to be completely sold out to Jesus? Do I want to have no further interest in living for myself? If that is what I want, I need to tell God now. And if that is not what I want, I need to tell God that as well.

If I ask God, he will bring me into an ever closer personal friendship with Jesus. Our friendship will be so dear to me that I will lose interest in the things of world. The things of this world are passing away. My relationship with God goes on forever!

Lord Jesus, I know it's not that the things in the "seen" world won't appeal to me—things like reading books, playing video games, sports, and fishing with Grandpa. But I really want my relationship with you to be so important that nothing else comes ahead of it. Draw me so close to you that nothing in this world attracts me as much as our friendship. Amen.

LIVE SECURE, AVOID DANGER

Set your minds on things above,
not on earthly things. For you died,
and your life is now hidden with Christ in God.

Colossians 3:2–3

I might think it is risky or foolish or unnecessary to follow Jesus. It is not. It is, at the same time, the safest and most adventuresome life I can possibly live. That's because I have almighty God in me and all around me.

The most dangerous thing is to try to live without God. I would much rather let my life be hidden in God than to hide from God and try to go it on my own.

— — — —

God, let my life be hidden in the shadow of your love. On this Christmas Eve, let the love of Jesus be born into the manger of my heart and let my life be a gift of his love to all those around me. Amen.

FROM OUTSIDE TO INSIDE

"The Lord himself will give you a sign:
The virgin will conceive and give birth to a son,
and will call him Immanuel."

Isaiah 7:14

Jesus came into this world from another world. He was born into this world. He was God in human flesh. In the same way, he wants to be born in me, in my heart.

Have I allowed my heart to become a "Bethlehem" for the Son of God? Has he been born in me?

— — — — —

Jesus, be born in me and let me be shaped and molded in your image. You grew from a baby in a manger into a boy and then a man who always pleased his heavenly Father. Help me grow into someone whose highest goal is to please you. Amen.

LIGHT IS MY FRIEND

Whatever is true, whatever is noble, whatever is right,
whatever is pure, whatever is lovely, whatever is
admirable—if anything is excellent or praiseworthy—
think about such things.

Philippians 4:8

The love of God is being poured into my heart by
the Holy Spirit. That is what turns me away from
everything that is not pleasing to him. The love of God
enables me to walk away from all that is dark (feelings like
anger, jealousy, and sadness). His love drives me closer to
the center of the light (what is pure and good and healthy).

When I come to the love of God, I come to the light.
There's no darkness in God.

━ ━ ━ ━

Jesus, in this season of dark mornings and wintry
weather, draw me ever closer to your light. Help me
turn away from anything that would bring darkness or
confusion into our relationship. Teach me how to walk
in the light of your love. Amen.

GOD, TAKE CONTROL

"To the one who is victorious and does my will
to the end, I will give authority over the nations."

Revelation 2:26

The most important battle I will ever fight is the battle for control of my life. That battle could happen quickly or it could take a long time. It's up to me.

I must get the question of who controls my life—God or me—settled once and for all. I must get alone with God and decide. Am I still fighting to run my own life? Or have I surrendered to God?

— — — — —

God, all I know is that I want to know you and serve you.
I want to love you, and I want to be my best for you. If
my stubbornness, selfishness, or forgetfulness gets in
the way of that, forgive me and bring my will back into
agreement with yours. Amen.

CHILDLIKE FAITH

"Truly I tell you, unless you change
and become like little children,
you will never enter the kingdom of heaven."

Matthew 18:3

I must be born from above (born again) to become God's child. But that is not a one-time experience. I need to come in childlike faith over and over again and be changed from my selfish ways into God's way of thinking.

A child can trust his earthly father to provide for him. So I can trust my heavenly Father to be the master of my life.

———

God, even as I grow up, keep me childlike in all the good ways, especially in my faith. Never let me lose my childlike confidence in you. You can provide for me, protect me, and show me the right path to follow for my life. Amen.

BETWEEN ME AND GOD

Do not think of yourself more highly than
you ought, but rather think of yourself
with sober judgment, in accordance
with the faith God has distributed to each of you.

Romans 12:3

I will walk in the light of the truth God shows me. I will try to never compare myself with others. I will try to never judge others. What others do is between them and God. What I do is between me and God.

I am accountable to him. I will try not to measure myself by any other standard than the standard made clear in the Word of God.

—————

God, sometimes it's so easy to be critical that I don't even realize I'm being critical. Also, I sometimes compare myself to other kids. I compare how smart I am, how far I can hit the ball, and whether I have lots of friends. Help me to be so focused on pleasing you that I lose sight of what others think of me. And help me to never compare myself to others or judge other kids. Amen.

THE REAL
SUPERMAN

Do not lie to each other, since you have
taken off your old self with its practices
and have put on the new self, which is being
renewed in knowledge in the image of its Creator.

Colossians 3:9–10

Jesus doesn't just want to patch up my natural self. He
wants to put a new supernatural self in me. He wants to
make me a new creation.

The Holy Spirit on the inside of me helps me to behave
like this new creation would behave. The Holy Spirit makes
me new from the inside out. The Holy Spirit in me has the
nature of Jesus. So, it will be "natural" for me to look more
and more like Jesus.

————

Jesus, make me new. Help me line up my behavior with
the new creation inside of me. Make me clean from
the inside out. Live within me and let me live today in
the truth that I am a new creation. Renew my mind so
that each day I understand more and more how I can
become like Jesus. Amen.

LIVING
FOR GOD TODAY

> But one thing I do: Forgetting what is behind
> and straining toward what is ahead, I press on toward
> the goal to win the prize for which God has
> called me heavenward in Christ Jesus.

Philippians 3:13–14

As the year ends, I might think about the mistakes and failures of the past year. I choose to let my past sins, mistakes, and failures be a reminder of the love and mercy of God. I trust him to guard me from repeating them in the new year.

God goes before me into the new year. Yesterday is past. Tomorrow isn't here yet. I trust him for today. He will keep me!

— — — — —

God, today is the only day I have. Yesterday is gone, and I can't do any yesterdays over again. Tomorrows are never a sure thing. But I have the gift of today. Help me. Make me new. And go with me into the coming year that I may be my best for you today, and every day. Amen.

ABOUT THE AUTHOR

Along with more than thirty years of experience in the publishing industry, Kent Garborg is an active volunteer in his church and is co-founder and president of Verus Community, a nonprofit organization providing mentoring, housing, and employment to men with a history of substance abuse. Kent and his beautiful wife, Betty, enjoy the precious gift of spending time with their children and grandchildren in Bloomington, Minnesota.